MARX AND ART

Insolubilia:
New Work in Contemporary
Philosophy

Series Editors: A. J. Bartlett, Justin Clemens and Jon Roffe

Insolubilia are problems that one cannot solve, cannot salve and cannot save — but which nonetheless cannot be avoided. This series publishes works that engage with the problems that deserve the name contemporary because they arise in and pertain specifically to our contemporary situation. These necessarily novel works will explore foundational questions in philosophy from a new perspective, offer new syntheses of previously disparate fields of investigation with an eye to the contemporary problematic, and think through in a rigorous way the relationship between previously heterogeneous concerns that now have come into contact (e.g., critical theory and the environment; philosophy and the market; neuroscience and poetry). Insolubilia is accordingly a series that publishes the latest works in continental philosophy that incarnate, present, and engage the insolubles of our time.

Mallarmé: Rancière, Milner, Badiou
Robert Boncardo and Christian R. Gelder

Marx and Art
Ali Alizadeh

MARX AND ART

Ali Alizadeh

**ROWMAN &
LITTLEFIELD**
INTERNATIONAL

London • New York

Published by Rowman & Littlefield International, Ltd.
6 Tinworth Street, London SE11 5AL
www.rowmaninternational.com

Rowman & Littlefield International, Ltd. is an affiliate of
Rowman & Littlefield
4501 Forbes Boulevard, Suite 200, Lanham, Maryland 20706, USA
With additional offices in Boulder, New York, Toronto (Canada), and
London (UK)
www.rowman.com

British Library Cataloguing in Publication Information
A catalogue record for this book is available from the British Library

ISBN: HB 978-1-7866-1011-9
ISBN: PB 978-1-7866-1012-6

Library of Congress Cataloging-in-Publication Data

Name: Alizadeh, Ali
ISBN: 978-1-78661-011-9 (cloth)
ISBN: 978-1-78661-012-6 (paperback)
ISBN: 978-1-78661-013-3 (electronic)

This book is dedicated to Jasper Pitt-Alizadeh

CONTENTS

ACKNOWLEDGEMENTS

I'd like to thank Anna MacDonald; the editors of *Insolubilia* – Justin Clemens, Adam Bartlett and Jon Roffe – and everyone at Rowman & Littlefield; Cindy Zeiher, for publishing an early version of aspects of this book in *Continental Thought & Theory*; and Tom Ford and Alex McDonald for their feedback on the manuscript-in-progress.

INTRODUCTION
Art – What Is It Good For?

ART, VALUE, AND THE CONTEMPORARY THINKER

In what must be one of the more convoluted policy statements spouted by a contemporary government officialdom, the United Kingdom's national body for funding and promoting the arts in England, Arts Council England, declares on its website that '[t]he value of arts and culture to people and society outlines the existing evidence on the contemporary impact of arts and culture on our economy, health and wellbeing, society and education'.[1]

It would require a good degree of fortitude and perseverance to untangle the meaning of this brazenly overwritten sentence. Note, for instance, the sheer opacity of the verb 'outline' in denoting the nature or substance of the relationship between 'the value of arts' and 'impact of arts'. This and other linguistic oddities of the statement – such as the perplexing formulation of saying that something in society outlines another thing in society – indicate that this sentence, as with other policy and politician-spoken statements of our era, is an exemplar in the craft of constructing elaborate verbal utterances without saying much at all.

However, if an unambiguous communication of its authors' understanding of the value of art is not one of the functions of this statement – an understanding which, at any rate, may be lacking in the first place – the combination of important-sounding nouns (*people, society, health,* and *education*) does convey the authors' general belief in the significance of art. The meaning of saying that the value of something *outlines* the evidence on the impact of that thing is utterly mysterious to me; but the desire of the speakers of this utterance to be seen to have something publicly and socially important to say on the topic is not so opaque. All modern democratic governments – and anti- or premodern autocrats too, for that matter – often wish to be seen to care about the value of art, even if articulating the reasons behind this desire is an insurmountable challenge for them, or at least for the English government.

The purpose of this book is not to mock politicians' – or, most probably, a poorly paid and overworked lower arts administrator's – ineptitude with written language. Indeed, semantic ambiguity and incomprehensibility may be a requirement of the genre of contemporary political communication, freeing the speaker from a difficult – and assessable – commitment to the message or promise of the statements made. At any rate, I do not wish to dwell any further on Art Council England's inability or unwillingness to articulate a view apropos of the question of the value of the arts. What I instead wish to focus on is the challenge of formulating a perspective regarding the value of art beyond alluding to a vague belief in the general *impact* of art on society and on societal motifs such as *health* and *education*.

And, importantly, this challenge is not at all unique to politicians and their copywriters. In the preface to a series of essays on the theme of artistic value published in *Arts21 Magazine*, the author has described both 'the relationship between art and money, and . . . the value of art in our individual lives' as 'deeply complicated'.[2] In an opinion piece published in the *Sydney Morning Herald*, the author Toni Hassan chides the Australian politicians whose laudable acknowledgement of the value of the arts – as seen in public statements uncannily similar to those of Arts Council England – have 'spruiked the economic benefits of the arts but said little about the delivery costs'.[3] Even a scholar of marketing and economics – who should, one would assume, be rather au fait at measuring the value and costs of things – such as Kim Lehman of Tasmanian School of Business and Economics isn't quite sure how to address this dilemma.[4] After distinguishing between the instrumental and intrinsic values or benefits of art, Lehman confuses the two terms by saying that both types of value must have discernible economic expressions if they are to be measurable and understandable. He claims that an example of the *instrumental* value of art may be seen in a public visual arts project which, in 'an economically depressed region' could result in 'increasing local employment'; but his example of the *intrinsic* value of art is also economic – he cites an instance of the evaluation of this kind of value in performing arts companies' desire to gauge audience satisfaction because the companies' 'revenue streams rely on a paying audience, and indeed one that returns for future performances'. One may forgive Lehman's preoccupation with all things financial as an aspect of his professional expertise, but his inability to truly differentiate between an instrumental and an intrinsic value of art – reducing both to the milieu of finance, capital and consumption – results in him failing to provide an answer to the question of art's value. He ends his piece by wondering if the true value of art can at all be discussed – by asking rhetorically, 'How do you measure intellectual stimulation? Emotional engagement?' – before concluding that perhaps 'the arts will continue to be valued more for its role as a driver of economic development than as a cure for the soul – or, worse still, not valued at all'.

It would be easy to be critical of an economist's seeming ineptitude in reflecting on art. And it would be fair to assume that if we are to discuss the value of art in the contemporary world, then we would surely be better off considering the perspectives of astute contemporary aestheticians and philosophers of art who have developed detailed theses apropos of the role and nature of art over the course of their long intellectual careers. But we may find that

it is not only economists or culture industry apparatchiks who
struggle with addressing the theme of artistic value, and that some
of today's most important philosophers also find it palpably difficult to explore the same theme. Indeed, it is in part due to such
difficulties that I have sought to find something like an answer to
this apparent quandary in the work of an earlier thinker born two
hundred years ago. But before attempting to establish why it is
this particular canonical thinker, the great Karl Marx, and not
another who is the subject of this book, I would first like to substantiate my claim regarding the challenge of talking about the
value of art in the milieu of contemporary philosophy. To this end,
I will briefly consider the theses of three of today's most central
philosophers of art.

Alain Badiou, Giorgio Agamben and Jacques Rancière began
publishing substantial book-length reflections on art from 1990s
onwards, and have arguably had more impact on the philosophical
investigation of art than the other thinkers of their generation.
Their works have marked a clear break with (so-called) postmod-
ernism, a trend which I would summarize as an intellectual – or
perhaps *anti*-intellectual – creed dedicated to disavowing the mo-
mentous commitments of earlier twentieth- and mid-twentieth-
century thinkers towards, among other things, the arts. Badiou,
Agamben and Rancière have not only opposed and in many ways
repelled the sophistry and frivolity of the *postmodern condition* by
writing seriously and substantially about art's power and specificity, they have also formulated a range of new influential concepts
and perspectives for exploring humanity's very old involvement in
making and thinking about art. And yet, when it comes to the
question of the value of art, these thinkers are not quite as helpful
as one may wish them to be.

Badiou, who also happens to be a practicing artist (a playwright
and a novelist), begins his 1998 book on art, *Handbook of Inaesthetics*, by posing a problem and proposing an agenda and a program. He believes that philosophy's historical relationship with art
has been analogous to the impasse between a hysteric and a master, an image borrowed from psychoanalysis.[5] Art is all presence,

aesthetic intensity and delusional pretense; philosophy, sober and desiring mastery over the beguiling hysteric, seems to have no choice but to either fall in love with or chastise art – 'the philosopher-master remains divided, when it comes to art, between idolatry and censure'.[6] Badiou sketches an outline of the Western philosophies of art, from ancient Greece to twentieth-century Europe, to suggest that the major philosophical schemata of theorizing the arts have been either censorious or *didactic*; idolatrous or *romantic*; or indifferent to the claims of art and hence classical or *aesthetic*. The philosopher who distrusts the very (artistic) charms that he or she is so fascinated by comes to see 'that art must be either condemned or treated in a purely instrumental fashion'.[7] Here Badiou is clearly, albeit indirectly, broaching the topic of value, by critiquing the *instrumental* view of art which, as we have seen, is one of the major frameworks for thinking about art's value. And, as such, according to the thinkers of this didactic, instrumentalist tradition, the value of art – or what Badiou describes as 'the "good" essence of art' – is to be found 'in its public effect, and not in the artwork itself'.[8] Badiou is quick to point out that this regime of thinking about art has found its polar opposite in another (romantic and, as it were, *proudly hysterical*) schema which vehemently rejects the didactic prism in favor of a view that assigns art what we might see as an excessively, insatiably immanent value – by claiming that 'art is the real body of truth'[9] – unamenable to attempts that seek to turn art into an instrument for bringing about a 'good' public effect. However, this perspective too fails to grant art a truly intrinsic value. According to the purveyors of this schema, the truth which the work of art embodies with such absoluteness is not unique or singular to the work, but it's 'the same truth that circulates' in philosophy.[10] Art's value, in other words, although seemingly defended against the skeptical master-philosopher, is in fact solely in its capacity for luminously revealing the truth, the same truth which is occulted elsewhere in, for example, philosophy or religion. As such, art is incapable of possessing *its own* truths and values, even according to the romantic *idolaters* who worship it. Finally, the last, classical schema, which neither prostrates before art nor banishes it, sees art's value – or 'the purpose' of art – in purely instrumental terms, as a 'therapeutic function' or a 'utility for the treatment of the affections of the soul'.[11]

I will attempt a somewhat similar and more detailed summary of Western philosophers' views of art later in this book. Badiou is correct, I think, to observe that so much of Western philosophy has been unable to see beyond the ways in which art can be utilized (for the public good, for individual therapy, for mystical revelation); but when it comes to proposing his own new, fourth schema which would afford art a fundamental and intrinsic – *immanent* and *singular*, in Badiou's parlance – *truth-producing* capacity or value, he oscillates between either praising the (particularly brilliant) artists' advent of (rather romantic or modernist) techniques for artistic 'differentiation'[12] which, in tandem with 'a principle of novelty',[13] result in 'distinctly perceivable works'[14] ; and valuing (rather didactically) 'a coresponsibility of art' to produce truths that are distinguishable from mere opinions.[15] I believe that groundbreaking works of art that launch new ways of making art, and also artworks that propose ideas that contradict common prejudices and doxa, are indisputably valuable. But neither of these values are intrinsic to the work of art and/or its making: to value the impact or consequences of a truly seminal (or, as Badiou would have it, *evental*) artistic act requires a study and knowledge of *other* works shaped by the original work's radical novelty; and, therefore, the work's value is not found in the artwork itself but in those that come after it. To acclaim art's – very occasional, one might add – capacity to defy public mores and dominant opinions strikes me as the master-philosopher's (no doubt sincere) enthusiasm for the artful hysteric's ability to shock and scandalize.

Published five years before Badiou's book, and by a European thinker highly conversant with Badiou's philosophy, Giorgio Agamben's *The Man Without Content* too names a problem and demands a solution vis-à-vis the modern appreciation of art. By citing a debate in nineteenth-century German philosophy, Agamben proposes that the main dialectic in our thinking about art concerns the tension and conflict between 'the aesthetic dimension' and 'the creative experience'.[16] It is common for scholars to lump aesthetic theory – which one may define as the philosophical investigation of the relationship between sense perception and subjectivity – together with the philosophy of art. As Agamben argues quite cogently, however, much of the modern philosophers' – and indeed many artists' own – views are highly critical of the fusion of a spectator's or a consumer's 'aesthetic enjoyment'[17] with the concerns of 'the one who produces'[18] art in the first place. Put in terms of the question of artistic value, we can say that for Agamben, art's intrinsic value is to be found in the creative act itself, prior to its creations being instrumentalized in the aesthetic dimension of consumption, criticism and commercialization. Agamben claims, quite emphatically, that

> [p]erhaps nothing is more urgent – if we really want to engage the problem of art in our time – than a destruction of aesthetics that would, by clearing away what is usually taken for granted, allow us to bring into question the very meaning of aesthetics as the science of the work of art. The question, however, is whether the time is ripe for such a *destruction*, or whether instead the consequence of such an act would not be the loss of any possible horizon for the understanding of the work of art and the creation of an abyss in front of it that could only be crossed with a radical leap. But perhaps just such a loss and such an abyss are what we most need if we want the work of art to reacquire its original stature.[19]

Towards the end of the book, and after having renounced the modern nihilism that condemns art to an 'interminable twilight',[20] Agamben advances a forceful thesis apropos of the original value or stature of art, which, he is quick to remind us, is not 'a cultural "value"'[21] if by value we mean only, as we often do in the modern world, a utilitarian or instrumental value. For Agamben, 'the gift of art'[22] is art's capacity to restore humanity to an original – one might say, *natural* and premodern – place in the world; art is 'for man the highest engagement, that is the engagement that keeps

him in the truth and grants to his dwelling on earth its original
status'.[23] However, even if we were to bring about or imagine a
destruction of the aesthetic (or the cultural) to pave the way for
the resurrection of this originary *gift of art*, we may still find that
'art will not simply be able to leap beyond its shadow to climb over
its destiny'.[24] Despite the urgency with which Agamben initially
implored us to do something about *the problem of art in our time*,
he concludes his book by reflecting on and valorizing melancholy
and nostalgia. If the aesthetic or instrumental valuation of art –
what Agamben refers to as 'the traditional value of the work of
art' – is to 'become unsteady', then this can only be done by making 'alienation from the past into a value'.[25] To transcend the
wasteland of aesthetic instrumentalization – or 'the desert of *terra
aesthetica*'[26] – art can only assume an otherworldly or angelic pos-
ture, whose 'melancholy is the consciousness that he [the mourn-
ful *angel of art*] has adopted alienation as his world; it is the nostalgia for a reality that he can possess only by making it unreal'.[27]

It would be quite easy to discern in Agamben's thesis of the
original stature of art the rather heavy presence of what Badiou
criticizes as a *romantic schema*. Even if art for Agamben has the
capacity to produce a *truthful* value contra the quotidian flounder-
ing of art and experience in *the desert* of consumption and judgement, this value is not intrinsic or unique – immanent and singular – to art, because it is concerned with *the* truth which is not an
artistic quality but (as something to do with *the original status of
man's dwelling on earth*) a clearly spiritual or metaphysical or
perhaps even New Ageist motif. Such a truth can, in other words,
be granted to us via means other than art – spirituality, religious
practices, yoga and so forth – and Agamben's approach, therefore,
can be said to depict art, however unintentionally, as an instrument that lacks its own singular truth or value. Furthermore, even
if this *gift of art* were an intrinsic value, the fact that, as Agamben
would have, it can only be granted to us via a melancholic detachment or alienation from the real world (of aesthetic debasement)
would imply that, whatever benefits it may bring us, it would be
nothing but *unreal* and abstract. How truly valuable would such

'phantasmagoric survival'[28] be vis-à-vis our concrete needs in the milieu of real (mental and physical) survival?

In the light of these concerns with Agamben's otherwise potent and provocative book, it may be salutary to now turn to the philosophy of Badiou's intellectual sparring partner, Jacques Rancière, a contemporary thinker who is openly appreciative, almost rapturous, about both the aesthetic and also about art's value in the modern world. Published in 2000 and following on from significant book-length publications on modern artists and literary writers, Rancière's *The Politics of Aesthetics: The Distribution of the Sensible* encapsulates and explicates the tenets of the philosopher's influential theory of art developed over three decades of reflecting on politics, education and society. Rancière notes, in the first place, that politics – which here assumes a classical definition concerning the dynamic of the constitution of legislative and executive powers within a community – has an inalienable visual and aural, that is, aesthetic, dimension: 'Politics revolves around what is seen and what can be said about it, around who has the ability to see and the talent to speak, around the properties of spaces and the possibilities of time'.[29] He then demarcates a place for art within politics' aesthetic center:

> It is on the basis of this primary aesthetics that it is possible to raise the question of 'aesthetic practices' as I understand them, that is forms of visibility that disclose artistic practices, the place they occupy, what they 'do' or 'make' from the standpoint of what is common to the community. Artistic practices are 'ways of doing and making' that intervene in the general distribution of ways of doing and making as well as in the relationships they maintain to modes of being and forms of visibility.[30]

While Rancière's evaluation of the aesthetic is radically different to Agamben's – for Rancière, the aesthetic, far from repressing art, expresses or *discloses* art – the two philosophers (although certainly not Badiou) have a basically similar definition of the aesthetic: it is the *common* space of sense perception (seeing and

hearing) which is not the same as, but certainly dialogic with, the
space of art (doing and making). And, in a dramatic disagreement
with both Badiou and Agamben, Rancière sees this commonality
as what is *common to the community* or *demos*. For Badiou and
Agamben – to different degrees and in quite different ways – the
aesthetic is imposed by or at least correspondent with the whims
of the society's elites; but for Rancière the aesthetic is inherently
democratic and is active in popular political and artistic practices
such as 'the assembly of artisans, inviolable written laws, and the
theatre as institution'.[31] However, the correspondence between
the aesthetic and the artistic (and the political) has not always
been of a highly democratic (in Rancière's sense of the word)
character; and, in a move that recalls Badiou's schematization,
Rancière proposes 'three major regimes' according to which art is
identified in the West.[32] These regimes are basically, although not
conclusively, historical, and each assigns an identity as well as a
function – and therefore value – to art in a given aesthetic context.
Under the *ethical regime of images*, while putatively concerned
with the arts' intrinsic value ('the question of their origin') alongside their instrumental value ('the question of their end or purpose'), art is ultimately assessed according to an instrumentalist
rubric that evaluates whether art can 'provide the spectator, both
children and adult citizens, with a certain education'.[33] In the
poetic regime of the arts, art, via representation and verisimilitude
in, for example, narrative drama and fiction, provides 'a relationship of global analogy with an overall hierarchy of political and
social occupations'.[34] Art as (political) analogy is an aesthetic instrument or a 'form of normativity' used by a highly hierarchical –
and hence un- or predemocratic – polity, and it too, therefore, has
mostly an instrumental value.

However, under the modern *aesthetic regime of the arts* (inau-
gurated with Romanticism and German Idealism in Europe) art
ceases to be an instrument for the upper casts of the society and,
furthermore, it ceases to be an instrument at all. Under this regime, according to Rancière, art is no longer laboriously divided
from the aesthetic, and one comes to discern 'a sensible mode of

being specific to artistic products'.[35] Agamben would, of course, not agree that whatever mode of sensation or sensibility a work of art might (temporarily) induce could ever amount to an *aesthetic regime*; but if such a thing were possible, then it may indeed equip the arts, as Rancière would have it, with an unprecedented emancipatory capacity and value: to 'free [art] from any specific rule, from any hierarchy of arts' and to enshrine both art as an intrinsic value – 'the autonomy of art' – and, in an extravagantly romantic equation, 'identify [art's] forms with the forms that life uses to shape itself'.[36] To reprise Badiou's disparagement of this kind of formulation, it is clear that here, according to Rancière's own account, *the forms of life itself* precede the (supposedly newly emancipated) forms of art, as it is the latter that (due to the event of the advent of the *aesthetic regime*) becomes identifiable with the former. So in a modern milieu in which art has been freed from either an ethical/educational or poetic/representational duty, art may be subordinated to the demands of a life seeking to *shape itself* (a use which, as with Agamben's theory of the truth, strikes me as an abstract mysticism, for example, as some kind of *selfspirituality*) which, at any rate, deprives art of a true autonomy or singularity as it once again puts art, by Rancière's own admission, at the service of 'the formation and education of a specific type of humanity'.[37]

None of this is to say that Rancière's theory of the fundamental difference in the relationship between the artistic and the aesthetic in the ancient, early modern and modern worlds is not compelling; or that Badiou and Agamben have not made highly pertinent and in many ways groundbreaking contributions to the contemporary philosophy of art. What I've attempted to show is that the artistic theories of three of the most influential contemporary philosophers of art are bedeviled by the challenge of assigning a value – be it a singularity, a truth content or a function – to the work and practice of art other than what we may see as (in many cases a rather abstract) instrumental value. It is for this reason that, in my attempt to propose and discuss a theory of value that would both overcome the simplicities – and perhaps insincerities – of the

mainstream technomanagerial arts industry as well as the problematic arguments of contemporary philosophical theorizing, I turn
to an older thinker, the most famous and also the most infamous
theorist of value in the history of philosophy, Karl Marx. Marx has,
of course, been abundantly praised and criticized for his theories
regarding both the material or economic and the ideological or
mental dimensions of our modern capitalist world. But can he
provide us with a theory of art, one which may help us better
understand, reframe and perhaps even – after Marx's own revolutionary ideals – transform the question of art's value?

APPROACHING MARX

I must state, from the outset, that the purpose of this book is not
to propose an economic-scientific method for calculating the value
of art à la some kind of (quasi-)Marxist agenda. I will not be
proposing a formula, for example, for estimating the portion of the
surplus-value extracted from the sale of a work of art commensu-
rate with the labour-time expended in the production of that work.
Such a task would require, above all else, that I assign to art only
(or at least primarily) an instrumental economic value – that is, to
focus on the exchange or monetized value of art or of artistic
labour-power – which, as we have seen, is something that even a
contemporary economist is not prepared and/or able to do. (As we
shall see, Marx himself would not accept that art could be seen in
such a way.) Furthermore, even if one were to make a philosophical concession to the contingency of commodification and capitalist economics, one may still struggle to assess art's (exchange-)
value in the same way that one would see the value of nonartistic
products. As artist and scholar Dave Beech has written in his recent book, *Art and Value*, 'art's mode of production [has] remained largely untouched by industrialisation and the transformation of handicraft into wage labour that was the bedrock of capitalist commodity production'.[38]

Nor do I wish, on the other hand, to make a case for art in exceedingly abstract, nonmaterialist terms that somehow exempt it altogether from the realities of our capitalist world and its determinations. Unlike what Beech goes on to do in his book, I will not base my arguments on a belief in art's exceptionality vis-à-vis market economics. While I agree that (some) artistic modes of production (e.g., writing, sculpting, etc.) have not been fundamentally altered by capitalist industrialization, I also note that art *can be* indeed very effectively – and profitably – commercialized and incorporated into the capitalist economy in many forms, such as financial investment in works by *bankable* artists in the art dealer market, or the gargantuan profits made from creative popular entertainment such as film, fashion and recorded music. As such, I must categorically reject, from the outset, immaterial and mystical views of art that propose to situate it outside of our modern socioeconomic conditions, even if such views do claim (quite erroneously, in my view) some kind of affinity with Marx's ideas. See, for example, the famous contemporary curator and art theorist Nicolas Bourriaud's influential late 1990s manifesto, *Relational Aesthetics*, which announces the sensational discovery of a somewhat utopian space for intrinsically, *socially valuable* artistic practice, one that is blissfully freed from the sordid businesses of the capitalist world, by (mis)representing a motif from Marx's *Capital, Volume One*:

> Over and above its mercantile nature and its semantic value, the work of art represents a social *interstice*. This *interstice* term was used by Karl Marx to describe trading communities that elude the capitalist economic context by being removed from the law of profit: barter, merchandising, autarkic types of production, etc. The interstice is a space in human relations which fits more or less harmoniously and openly into the overall system, but suggests other trading possibilities than those in effect within this system.[39]

It is correct that Marx does use the term *interstice*, but that's unfortunately all that is correct about Marx in Bourriaud's description. According to Marx, the interstitial communities, far from eluding or being somehow external to the capitalist economy, were in fact *the very genesis of capitalism* in (parts of) the precapitalist ancient world. To demonstrate the extent of Bourriaud's mistake – with the intention of highlighting the deep problem with a contemporary theory of artistic value that flagrantly ignores history, politics and economics at the service of a putatively *progressive anticapitalist* agenda and its dreamy *other possibilities* – I would like to quote the relevant passage from *Capital, Volume One* in which Marx brings up the topic of interstice:

> In the Asiatic and other ancient modes of production, we find that the conversion of products into commodities, and therefore the conversion of men into producers of commodities, holds a subordinate place, which, however, increases in importance as the primitive communities approach nearer and nearer to their dissolution. Trading nations, properly so called, exist in the ancient world only in the interstices, like the gods of Epicurus in the Intermundia, or like Jews in the pores of Polish society. Those ancient social organisms of production are, as compared with bourgeois society, extremely simple and transparent. But they are found either on the immature development of man's individually, who has not yet severed the umbilical cord that unites him with his fellowmen in a primitive tribal community, or upon direct relations of subjection.[40]

Against Bourriaud's reading of Marx, we must note that for Marx the interstice was absolutely not the zone for a primitive autarkic economy but the first – *immature, simple and transparent* – stage in *the severance of the umbilical cord that unites people with primitive tribal community*. It seems that Bourriaud, by misappropriating a Marxian theme, wishes to embellish the very lucrative and by all accounts ruthless contemporary art market (of which he himself is a direct proponent and beneficiary) with the aura of an innocent, early precapitalist mercantile community of happy barterers. For Marx himself, however, such a community, while subordinate to the dominant existing mode of production (e.g. the mercantile Jews in the mostly agricultural Poland), was also at the historical forefront of undermining or *dissolving* feudalism by ushering in the more advanced era of *the conversion of products into commodities, and therefore the conversion of men into producers of commodities*, that is, the age of capitalism. The interstice may be in some sense outside or on the margins – or, more accurately and interestingly, within the invisible, shadowy *pores* – of the materiality of the dominant economic conditions and, as such, it might be akin to the ancient materialist philosopher Epicurus's concept of Intermundia, a cosmic space (relatively) empty of physical matter. But, as with Intermundia – which, according to the ancient philosopher, becomes the abode of gods – in the history of humanity the socioeconomic interstice becomes the birthplace of the new gods of the *direct relations* of the market and commodification.

I would like to emphasize that my aim in showing the blatant problems with Bourriaud's enlistment of Marx in his valorization of postmodernist curatorial practice has been made in part in the interest of showing that if we are to consult Marx about the question of art's value, we must be wary of existing accounts of Marx's thought – even by supposedly sympathetic *leftist* commentators such as Bourriaud – and return to Marx's own writings. This principle is at the heart of this book. Much has of course been written on what is assumed to have been Marx's position on art – and I shall consider the key works of this tradition in the conclusion to this book and evaluate them in terms of what I will argue to be Marx's own position on art – but there exist very few sustained, book-length explorations of his thinking about art based solely on his own words and writings. Much of the postulations of contemporary (so-called) Marxist literary theory, for example, are based on assumptions of other Marxist literary theorists and not on Marx's own writings on art. (A typical, well-known example of this kind of work is Tony Bennett's popular 1979 textbook *Formalism and Marxism* which claims, quite unapologetically, that 'more im-

portant' than 'Marx's writings on art and literature' are 'the major
schools of Marxist criticism'.[41]) These assumptions have led to
limited, and in some cases, erroneous conclusions, far more egre-
gious than Bourriaud's misreading, such as the view that Marx did
not have much to say about the arts; or that he saw art solely as a
bourgeois or ruling class ideological phenomenon; or that the only
kind of artistic practice compatible with his thought is one which is
didactically political or propagandistic.

This book argues that, by returning to Marx's actual writings,
from his juvenile poetry and earliest journalism to his final publications, we may discover a theory which not only challenges many
tenets of contemporary Marxist (and otherwise) literary or cultural
theory, but one which also presents us with a profound, coherent
and stimulating theory of art that defines, values and demonstrates
artistic practice. By mapping Marx's intellectual development
from the ideals of a young Hegelian to the polemics of a seasoned
internationalist communist, I aim to show that Marx, despite his
often-violent clashes with his surrounding social and intellectual
circles, and his lifelong construction of a contrarian and mostly
singular approach to the questions of consciousness and society,
never lost sight of art as a key aspect of human activity.

By arguing against the perception that Marx's proper emergence as a political theorist entailed a conclusive break with all
kinds of humanism, I will illustrate that, by merging the Hegelian
accounts of production and art as an end-in-itself with tropes of
modern economic theory (most significantly the differentiation
between use-value and exchange-value), Marx was able to provide
an important and compelling account of art, one which sees art as
possessing the capacity for the production of *intrinsic use-value*.
Marx's materialist take on the theme of alienation, and his ability
to extract a key nonutilitarian element from Aristotle's perception
of human capacity, provided him with the tools for proposing that
art is the practice (and not the outcome) of producing unalienating
theoretical or mental objects or artworks.

By referencing a variety of Marx's writings and closely analyz-
ing an array of passages – some of which have never been analyzed

in the context of a study of Marx's philosophy of art – I aim to establish that for Marx art is a material and sociohistorically situated activity which produces values that respond to actual needs and impulses of humanity. I shall emphasize that, contra Aristotle, these needs are neither anterior to or outside of specific modes and relations of exploitative productions, and that, for Marx, our mental or theoretical needs are very much necessitated by the fetishism and ideology of specific modes and relations of production. Art is the transformation of the dark, alienating power and dominance of ideology (be it mythology, religion or capitalist hegemony) into comprehensible, unfrightening objects; and, as such, in its unity of *poiesis* and *praxis*, art is the activity which allows us to understand the world and perhaps even understand how we may change it.

This is not to say that under the aegis of capitalism, both during Marx's life and our own, art has visibly and publicly retained its value. Art has been, needless to say, debased and instrumentalized. My discussion and analysis of (what I shall posit as) Marx's philosophy of art has been framed by an analysis of the discourse of value in contemporary cultural scenes, and I shall suggest ways in which this discourse may be revised and hopefully rethought in the light of my understanding of Marx's theory of art. It is also hoped that this book will enable us to address some of the complexities and difficulties found in the theories of contemporary philosophers such as Badiou, Rancière and Agamben. By proposing ways in which a labour theory of artistic value could enrich these thinkers' thoughts, I aim to contribute to current debates in contemporary philosophy by giving an account of art as envisaged by one of the modern world's most influential thinkers.

NOTES

1. Arts Council England, 'The Value of Arts and Culture to People and Society', *Arts Council England*, accessed 21 July 2017, http://www.

artscouncil.org.uk/exploring-value-arts-and-culture/value-arts-and-culture-people-and-society .

2. Nicole J. Caruth, 'What Is the Value of Art?' *Art21 Magazine*, 28 May 2014, accessed 21 July 2017, http://magazine.art21.org/2014/05/28/flash-points-what-is-the-value-of-art/.

3. Toni Hassan, 'How Do You Put a Value on Art, and the People Creating It?' *The Sydney Morning Herald*, 9 March 2016, accessed 21 July 2017, http://www.smh.com.au/comment/how-do-you-put-a-value-on-art-and-the-people-creating-it-20160308-gne4sc.html .

4. Kim Lehman, 'The Tricky Notion of "Value" in the Arts', *The Conversation*, 24 November 2013, accessed 21 July 2017, http://theconversation.com/the-tricky-notion-of-value-in-the-arts-20408 .

5. Alain Badiou, *Handbook of Inaesthetics*, trans. Alberto Toscano (Stanford: Stanford University Press, 2005), 1.

6. Ibid, 2.

7. Ibid.

8. Ibid, 3.

9. Ibid.

10. Ibid, 7.

11. Ibid, 4.

12. Ibid, 10.

13. Ibid, 12.

14. Ibid, 13.

15. Ibid, 15.

16. Giorgio Agamben, *The Man Without Content*, trans. Georgia Albert (Stanford: Stanford University Press, 1999), 2.

17. Ibid, 4.

18. Ibid, 5.

19. Ibid, 6. Note that the emphasis in this passage and all emphases in all other quotations in this book appear as such in the original texts and have not been added by me.

20. Ibid, 58.

21. Ibid, 101.

22. Ibid.

23. Ibid, 102.

24. Ibid, 103.

25. Ibid, 105.

26. Ibid, 102.

27. Ibid, 110.

28. Ibid, 111.

29. Jacques Rancière, *The Politics of Aesthetics*, trans. Gabriel Rockhill (London: Bloomsbury, 2011), 8.

30. Ibid.

31. Ibid, 9.

32. Ibid, 16.

33. Ibid.

34. Ibid, 17.

35. Ibid, 18.

36. Ibid, 19.

37. Ibid.

38. Dave Beech, *Art and Value: Art's Economic Exceptionalism in Classical, Neoclassical and Marxist Economics* (Leiden: Brill, 2015), 11.

39. Nicholas Bourriaud, *Relational Aesthetics*, trans. Simon Pleasance and Fiona Woods (Dijon: Les presses du réel, 2009), 16.

40. Karl Marx, *Capital*, ed. David McLellan (Oxford: Oxford University Press, 2008), 49–50.

41. Tony Bennett. *Formalism and Marxism* (London: Methuen & Co. Ltd., 1979), 101.

I

ART AND VALUE BEFORE MARX

I would like to begin by sketching an outline of some of the key theories of art prior to Marx. My intention is to both ground Marx's approach and discoveries in the works of philosophers who directly influenced him – Marx's fellow-German near contemporary Hegel, most notably – and set the parameters of Marx's specific discussion in the terms proposed by the tradition of Western philosophy – a tradition which, despite Marx's nonphilosophical political and economic commitments and interests, is arguably the first and foremost context for the manifestation of his own ideas. I will read these philosophers' views with a focus on their conceptions of *use* and *value* in art. I will suggest, via reading Book X of the *Republic*, that Plato dismisses the instrumental value of art and advocates art's – very rare – intrinsic capacity to make claims to truth; that, in the *Poetics*, Aristotle detects a universalizing value in art's cathartic capacity, a value which is, nevertheless, immediately subsumed into an ethical paradigm; that Rousseau believes, in *A Discourse on the Moral Effects of Arts and Sciences*, that art has a transcendent intrinsic value which is greatly corrupted and turned parasitic due to the aesthetic preoccupations of modern society; that Kant argues, in the *Critique of Judgement*, that art has an inherent worth in advancing mental and cognitive powers, but he does not deem art useful because he sees *use* as limited to the sphere of the physical; and Hegel claims, in his *Lectures on Aesthetics*, that art has a spiritual value but he too does not view art as useful because he sees any kind of use as a form of instrumentalization which would undermine art's true, transcendent potential.

While, as we have seen, so much of the discussions of the value of art in our own contemporary late capitalist world is almost entirely focused on the monetary (instrumental) value of art – either to do with funding for the arts, artists' pay, or art as either investment or as commodity – in much of the canon of Western philosophy, and as seen in my summary of the theories of three contemporary philosophers – the dominant discussions of art have been premised upon attempts at describing, either appreciatively or critically, the innate, inalienable and hence non- or precommercial value or qualities of art. This is not to say that Western thinkers have endeavored to see art as intrinsically *useful* in the common understanding of the word – that is, as something with ostensibly, concretely beneficial qualia – but that they have sought to depict the value of art (be it a positive or a negative value) as a quality inherent and specific to the work's immanent manifestation, and not as an outcome determined by (secondary, nonphilosophic configurations of) its sociocultural evaluation.

Indeed, in what can be described as the first serious and perhaps most foundational discussion of art in Western philosophy – Book X of Plato's *Republic* – art is presented as very much *useless* and also *valueless* precisely because it is, according to Plato, devoid of an instrumental value. After arguing that all art is more or less a genus of representation, and that all representation is quite far removed from reality, Plato asserts that the supreme literary creator of the ancient Hellenic world, Homer, would not be able to 'explain medicine or any similar skilled activity to us' even if he is able to 'imitate doctors' talk' in his poetry.[1] This allows Plato to advance that the poet, therefore, has no 'practical skill' and can do 'no public service'.[2] To substantiate this potentially scandalous view of a much-loved poet, Plato argues that the key reason for the artist's inability to perform an ostensibly beneficial task in society is that, in representing objects such as the horse's bit and bridle or a human subject such as the harness-maker – in, presumably, a poem or a painting with an equestrian subject – the artist displays, in addition to an ignorance apropos the practical skill required for making the bit and bridle, no knowledge of how to *use* the represented objects because 'only a horseman . . . knows how to use them'.[3] This brings Plato to conclude, in this part of his observation on the arts, that 'the artist knows little or nothing about the subjects he represents and that his art is something that has no serious value'.[4]

Before trying to unravel what Plato means by *serious value* – something that I believe is actually quite different to an instrumental value – let us note that he has limited his conception of *use* to the sphere of professional practice and that he does not see it connected, as Marx will later insist, to the sphere of general human needs. The bridle or the flute (one of Plato's other famous examples) are only useful to the horseman and to the flutist, and it is therefore only these ascribed users who can truly know the value of the object, not the artists who paint pictures or write poems about bridled horses and flutes and also, interestingly, not even the producers of the bridle and the flute, the harness-maker or the flute-maker. In other words, for Plato, use is very much conflated with consumption and also with an instrumental social benefit. The supposed resulting uselessness of art, however, is not Plato's major concern with art. Later in the *Republic*, he argues that art, while benefit-less and useless, is not entirely ineffective, for it appeals to an 'inferior' dimension of the human subject which the philosopher would 'call irrational and lazy and cowardly'.[5] This claim leads to Plato's 'gravest charge against poetry', his accusing poetry – and, by extension, all art – of having 'a terrible power to corrupt even the best characters' as it draws us (the consumers or, in Plato's sense, users of poetry and art) into a vortex of sinister, excessive emotionality – 'the poet gratifies and indulges the natural instinct to give full vent to our sorrows' and diverts us from 'the interests of our own welfare and happiness'.[6]

What are we to make of the *terrible power* of art if we are to also acknowledge its uselessness and valuelessness? Can't such a power be seen as a kind of value – insofar as both power and value denote a capacity or the means for developing a capacity – or can't such a destructive power actually have its uses (against, say, an enemy)? Detecting the creeping emergence of a contradiction in his polemic against art, Plato ends this discourse by acknowledging somewhat begrudgingly, albeit unambiguously, that there are a few instances in which poetry may be seen to have an instrumental potential – 'hymns to the gods and paeans in praise of good men'[7] – and that he would be open to hearing poetry's defenders argue that poetry 'brings lasting benefits to human life and human society'.[8] Plato claims, however sincerely, that he 'shall be glad if [art and/or poetry] proves to have a real value', although, until such a time as this proof has been offered – and accepted by the hard-nosed philosopher – he will insist that 'poetry has no serious value or claim to truth'.[9]

We can now understand what Plato means by *real* or *serious value* when it comes to art and poetry. Instrumentally beneficial artistic products – such as religious songs and moral tales – may be allowed in Plato's ideal society despite art's generally and/or mostly harmful capacity, but whatever (supposedly minor and ephemeral) sociomoral benefits are to be accrued from such an allowance, these are not real or serious values. To bring *lasting* benefits to society, art must make *a claim to truth* instead of either representing people and things (doctors, bits and bridles, etc.) or indulging in overt, obsessive sentimentality and aestheticized pathology. Plato does not elaborate on how art may make a claim to truth, or what species of truth would be considered artistic, but it seems clear that for him the real and serious value of art would be an intrinsic value, because any claim to truth is entirely immanent to the claim itself or, in this case, to the work of art, prior to the societal and extrinsic instrumentalization of the truths to which the work has made claims. Put differently, for Plato, art's value – illusive, rare and perhaps impossible as it may be – can be established if and when art is shown to possess not power per se but the power to produce truths and knowledge à la science and perhaps philosophy itself.

Plato's student and the next major Western philosopher to offer a significant theory of art and of artistic value, Aristotle, is
much less interested in making a case for the truthfulness of art
than in arguing that the very (fundamental) artistic powers which
Plato found so terrible – art's powerful appeal to emotion as opposed to reason – are in fact useful. Aristotle writes, in the *Poetics,*
that, despite Plato's renunciation of supposedly valueless artistic
representations, the most basic unit or *technē* of representation –
imitation – is something that 'comes naturally to human beings
from childhood' and so does 'the universal pleasure in imita-
tions'.[10] Interestingly, this pleasure is not an end in itself, but the
means for us 'to understand and work out'[11] the subject or the real
world signified or imitated in the work of art. Art, then, can be said
to have the use of providing us with an accessible, aesthetic medium for coming to terms with the world. Aristotle also, famously,
proposes that art – or, more specifically, tragic drama – has the
capacity for 'effecting through pity and fear the purification of
such emotions' in an audience;[12] and that the art of poetry even
possesses the capacity to be 'more philosophical and more serious'
than the work of a historian because the poet's function is not to
simply 'say what *has* happened, but to say the kind of thing that
would happen'.[13]

From a contemporary perspective, the theme of *the purification of undesirable emotions* or catharsis may be best approached
through a psychoanalytic prism. But, for the purposes of setting
the context for Marx's intervention in the Western philosophy of
art, I'd like to emphasize that Aristotle's take on imitation, whatever the structure of its psychosemantic function may be, grants art a
use and a positive value denied to it by Plato. For Aristotle, imitation is an inalienable aspect of the nature of our species, and
participation in it has universalizing consequences, qualities
which, as we shall see, Marx will find in the act of production.
Furthermore, for Aristotle, art has the power to counter the feelings of *distress* – which may be seen to anticipate *alienation* –
engendered by the fearsomeness of our reality. When discussing
the universal pleasure of artistic imitation, Aristotle proposes that

'we take delight in viewing the most accurate possible images of
objects which in themselves cause distress when we see them
(e.g., the shapes of the lowest species of animals [by which Aristotle most probably means spiders, snakes and scorpions], and
corpses)'.[14] As such, art has the value of helping us overcome the
terror and abjection aroused by what seems grotesque to us, and it
can be valued for its capacity to produce delight in place of fear in
the human subject. And, therefore, the cathartic function has a
(psychoethical) purpose beyond the artistic. *Purification of emotions* and what we experience *when we see* art are the topoi of
sensory or aesthetic apperception of artistic creation (by audiences
and, indeed, by some philosophers), and they are not inherent to
the *work* – either the process or the object – of art. *Pleasure in
imitation* may indeed hold some value for some artists, but it's
clearly not a sensation either intrinsic or singular to art, as neither
pleasure nor imitation are solely artistic phenomena and can be
found in nonartistic contexts. As such, while in opposition to Plato,
Aristotle does render some of the qualia of art valuable, he grants
art only a nonintrinsic value based primarily on the effect the arts
may have on some of their consumers.

Plato's and Aristotle's influences on Western theories of art
would remain central, and it was not until the emergence of Romanticism and German Idealism that different and new perspectives on the nature and value of art would again be proposed by
Western philosophers. As Badiou has noted, 'the question of art'
did not 'torment' medieval and early modern thinkers such as
Descartes, Leibniz or Spinoza.[15] During this period, art and art's
value were mostly understood in ways that combined Platonic and
Aristotelian elements. In the *Confessions* of Augustine of Hippo,
for example, the renowned theologian seems very much a Platon-
ist – or, more accurately, a Neoplatonist – when he derides his
younger self's teaching of 'the art of public speaking' as a profession, for 'love of money'.[16] The problem, according to Augustine,
is not one's pursuit of a profession and/or the intimation of greed
per se, but that, by treating an artistic skill as a useful profession –
by selling 'to others the means of coming off the better in de-

bate'[17] – one will undermine truth itself. By teaching *the art of public speaking*, despite one's reasonable intention to simply have a profession that benefits others in the community, one cannot help but teach 'the tricks of pleading' and assist others with 'their futile designs and their schemes of duplicity' which may be used, in a judicial context, to violate truth and 'get the innocent condemned'.[18] Here, the artist – or the one who assigns an artistic practice a social value by turning that practice into a profession – in a misguided attempt to render art useful, turns art into a *trick* that can undermine the (Platonic) potential for art's *real* and *serious* value. Augustine, however, it not nearly as dogmatically opposed to art as one may expect from a Neoplatonist Christian thinker – and a future Catholic saint – as we also find the echo of Aristotle's defense of art in the *Confessions*. While advancing an aesthetic theory of visual beauty – according to which visible things can be divided into 'two classes, those which please the eye because they are beautiful in themselves and those which do so because they are properly proportioned in relation to something else'[19] – he suggests that this theory can be applied to 'material forms' with 'line and color and shape',[20] among which we may place works of (visual) art. And yet this artistic beauty is not necessarily a falsifying trick, but the harbinger of 'the peace that virtue brings' and a proof of the connection between 'goodness' (with all its religious connotations) and artistic or compositional 'unity', that is, proportionality and harmony.[21] Although Augustine is quick to emphasize that the origin of all artistic beauty – and of artistic ugliness or 'discord' and 'disunion' too, for that matter[22] – is god and that all reflections on art and aesthetics should ultimately be abandoned in favor of reflections on god, his appreciation of beauty and its peaceful effects on the soul convey something of Aristotle's theory of catharsis.

The idea of god as such or something not so unlike god retains its connection with the question of art in the work of the first major modern Western philosophers of art, and it's not until Marx himself, perhaps, that it becomes possible to propose an explicitly materialist theory of art. In one of his first published works, *A*

Discourse on the Moral Effects of Arts and Sciences, Jean-Jacques
Rousseau scolds earlier rationalist philosophers for their claim that
'nothing exists but matter and that there is no God but the
world'.[23] Interestingly, Rousseau's impassioned denunciation of
such (supposedly atheist) thinkers as Hobbes and Spinoza entails a
categorization of their writings as a form of art or, more
(melo)dramatically, as 'the baneful arts of our forefathers'.[24] This
important assimilation of philosophers and artists marks a significant break with Plato and could be seen as one of the hallmarks of
Romanticism. And yet, much of what Rousseau says about art may
seem very similar to Plato's condemnation of poetry. Rousseau
claims that 'our souls have been corrupted in proportion as our
sciences and arts have advanced toward perfection' – note another
un-Platonic formulation, the grouping of arts and sciences together – and that, historically speaking, 'the progress of the arts [and]
the dissolution of morals' work in tandem.[25] As an illustration of
the art's immoralism, Rousseau explains how art (or, more specifically, the very subject of Augustine's complicated contempt, the
art of rhetoric) has 'taught our passions to speak an artificial language' and has undermined our 'natural' propensity for seeking
'security in being able to discern each other's feelings and intentions'.[26] The devices and flourishes of the art of public speaking
have turned direct, honest communication – 'whose values we no
longer appreciate'[27] – into a medium for sycophancy, sophistry
and falsehood. As such, it should not surprise us that, according to
Rousseau, 'evils flow from literature and the arts'.[28]

It might seem strange that Rousseau, himself a committed literary writer, would hold such a negative view of art and that he
would find *values* only in the nonartistic and see art as antagonistic
towards such values. But a closer reading of *A Discourse* would
find, beyond the hyperbolic and, indeed, rhetorical style of Rousseau's writing, a deeper and much more original account of art,
one which argues in favor of (a new and potentially revolutionary)
art. Early in his celebrated essay, Rousseau observes that 'the
mind has its needs, as well as the body' before elaborating that
while the modern human is *bodily* constrained and enchained by

'despotic' politics, literature and the arts contribute to this oppression *mentally* and 'strew garlands of flowers on the iron chains'.[29] It is important to note that before art becomes an instrument for hiding the mechanics of unjust politics and deceiving the people, it possesses the capacity to answer our natural mental *needs*. Rousseau does not explain what these needs may be, but at no point does he deny their existence nor does he actually decry the need for the existence of art. What he is much more explicitly critical of are the social conditions that turn art into a source of corruption. Offering one of the first instances of a socioeconomic critique in the context of a discourse on the arts, Rousseau observes that art's *evil* manifestation as luxury – associated with 'idleness and vanity of men' – is due to the specific symbolic order of a modern society in which luxury is 'regarded as a sure sign of wealth'.[30] In other words, art is reduced to the status of luxury – which, in turn, has a negative effect on morals – not because of there being anything intrinsically immoral in art, but due to the social system in which wealth is paramount and compels an irresistible demand for luxury items. In what anticipates both nineteenth-century – and, indeed, our own contemporary – capitalism and Marx's attack on it, Rousseau observes that this particular corruption of art can only happen in a society in which 'a man's worth to the state is only that of what he consumes'.[31]

As such, it is not art but luxury which results in 'the dissolution of morals', which 'in turn brings about the corruption of taste'.[32] In a sharp break with Aristotle, and inaugurating the modern disjunction between art and aesthetics (as revived in Agamben's recent works), Rousseau depicts the aesthetic dimension of modern (capitalist) society as that which devalues and degrades art. An artist who has 'the misfortune' of living where 'the tone of the society' is set by *the corrupted taste* of 'the frivolous' and 'the fainthearted' can only 'produce commonplace works that will be admired during his lifetime, rather than marvels that would not be admired until long after his death'.[33] As such, we may say that for Rousseau, art is intrinsically valuable – contra its instrumentalization as luxury – if it possesses an artistic timelessness or, put simply, *gen-*

ius. Towards the end of his essay, Rousseau tempers his polemic by allowing that 'a few men' – those possessing 'vast genius' – may be exempt from his (often) unrelenting attack on the arts (of his society), those 'capable of raising monuments to the glory of the human mind'.[34] These few exemptions notwithstanding, and for reasons already mentioned (e.g., the corruption of human nature under modern consumerist social relations), Rousseau maintains that it is best for most (i.e., nongenius) people to desist from aspiring to enter 'the Temple of the Muses', for it is far better to do something that is 'useful to society'; for example, it is better to be 'an outstanding cloth manufacturer' than 'a bad versifier'.[35] For Rousseau, while art can – under quite rare circumstances of *vast artistic genius* – result in something of *monumental* value, it more commonly contributes to a further dissolution of morals, and is, therefore, not a useful thing.

Although ostensibly influenced by Rousseau, Immanuel Kant, the next major European thinker to write substantially about art, does not see the topic of art as inflected by social or economic conditions. In his *Critique of Judgment*, and in a move that resonates with Aristotle and also, rather strongly, with the Aristotelian aspects of Christian thinkers such as Augustine, the aesthetic and its associated themes such as beauty, taste and judgement become a nonsocial, immaterial and transtemporal category, associated with quasi-divine notions such as the Sublime. However, Kant does allow for a functional division between art itself – which in Kant and in much of the German Idealist tradition is referred to as *fine art* to differentiate between *fine* artistic production (e.g., poetry) and *mechanical* artisanal production (e.g., pottery) – and the aesthetic. According to him, 'for *judging* beautiful objects, as such, what is required is *taste*; but for fine art, i.e., the *production* of such objects, one needs *genius*'.[36] Kant's introduction of the topic of *production* into the Western philosophy of art is crucial, not only for the next generations of German thinkers such as Marx, but also with regard to the question of art's value. It is in the context of seeing the work of art as a product – of an artist's 'often laborious', 'slow and even painful process of improvement, directed to making the form adequate to his thought'[37] – that art can be said to have a *use*. Here, the work of the genius – which in Rousseau and much of Romanticism may be said to have an undefinable, abstract quality – acquires a definition and a specificity. Kant sees such a work as 'a model' that, in the objectivity of its 'execution' and as a 'product', can transmit *the rule* of creative methods of making art – as an artist's 'only means of handing down' artistic skills – 'which others [e.g., the artist's pupils] may use to put their talents to test'.[38]

It may be said that this value of the work of art – as a concrete and analyzable model to be used 'not for *imitation*, but for *following*'[39] by one's pupils – is pedagogic, and, as such, not truly or singularly artistic. But it should be noted that this educational use is limited to the sphere of artistic production. Unlike the (very few) civic and moral educational uses that Plato saw (in even fewer) genres of art, for Kant works of artistic genius 'can do no more than furnish rich *material* for products of fine art',[40] and they do not at all make contributions to the general, nonartistic milieu. Kant is in fact openly contemptuous of the 'ridiculous' 'impostor' who might 'pass sentence like a genius in matters that fall to the province of the most patient rational investigation', meaning, in the province of the nonartistic (e.g., the scientific).[41] And yet it also cannot be said that the nonimpostor or the authentic artistic genius – the artist or the work of art that garners an artistic following (or an *artistic configuration*, as Badiou might have it) – possesses an intrinsic artistic value, even if this value is specific to the work and world of art. This is because, as noted above, the exemplary work of art, when *used* as a model by less skilled or novice artists, is only a *means* or an instrument for conveying *the rule* of art, and not an *end* in itself. While Kant's description of art as material production is key to understanding Marx's theories, it should also be noted that for Kant *use* can only imply instrumentalization, and if art has an intrinsic value, then it is to be found not in the sphere of production, but in what Kant ultimately sees as the more important and determinant spheres of consumption and perception.

Kant is quite open to acknowledging art's value – even its deeper, supposedly intrinsic value – but only insofar as art is brought back under the aegis of *taste* and *judgement*, or, the aesthetic. He claims that art is 'intrinsically purposive' and has 'the effect' – and not the intended use – 'of advancing the culture of the mental powers in the interests of social communication'[42] ; and that 'we measure the worth of the fine arts by the culture they supply to the mind'.[43] But it is quite clear that, for such a *worth* to be intrinsic to the work of art, it can only be *measured* – if indeed such an outlandishly intangible thing as *advancing the culture of the mental powers* can be measured at all – from the perspective of the *tasteful* nonproducer or the judge of art, whose mind may become more cultured thanks to (the effects of) art. And, if it is only for the producers of art – who, according to Kant, see art only as a *means* – that art has a *use*, then for the discerning and judgemental general nonartistic public who value art for its being an *end-in-itself*, art can have no use whatsoever. As such, and despite Kant's clear enthusiasm for art, it is not literature or music but 'mechanical art' which he can confidently call 'useful'.[44]

The final philosopher whose theory of art I'd like to briefly note prior to exploring Marx's thoughts on art is a thinker who responded to Plato's and Aristotle's foundational theories of art and who also was directly influenced by Kant and in turn directly influenced Marx's philosophy. In his *Introductory Lectures on Aesthetics*, Georg Wilhelm Friedrich Hegel considers and finds insufficient both the Platonic view – which, by presenting art as 'the purely formal imitation of what we find given . . . can bring to the birth only *tricks* and not *works* of art'[45] – and the Aristotelian defense of imitation, because 'the doctrine of the purification of passion suffers indeed under the same defect'[46] as the Platonic position. In both cases, according to Hegel, 'the purpose of art' has been 'limited' to that of 'utility' – or that of a pure instrument – and 'its conception is rooted in something else, to which it is a *means*'.[47] Hegel's own project consists of a theory of artistic value which views art as *an end in itself*, and I believe, his most important contribution in this regard is to propose that art (and not only its aesthetic effect, as Kant would have it) possesses a genuinely intrinsic value. Hegel, in other words, proposes that art has a *real and serious value* vis-à-vis Plato's injunction. And, also important-ly, Hegel builds on Rousseau by specifying (somewhat) the human needs that art seeks to satisfy. Such needs are, for Hegel, 'the higher needs'[48] and their satisfaction in a work of art produces 'spiritual value'.[49]

It is important not to conflate Hegel's view of art as a capacity for producing *spiritual value* with Plato's (minimal) interest in religious cultural products such as hymns. For Hegel, even an explicitly spiritual art should not be seen to 'have value as a useful instrument in the realization of an end having substantive impor-tance *outside* the sphere of art',[50] such as moral or religious educa-tion. Art should instead be seen to have 'the vocation of revealing *the truth* in the form of sensuous artistic shape' and 'having its purpose in itself'.[51] So, unlike Aristotle and Kant but in agreement with Plato and Augustine, Hegel sees *truth* as a key criterion to which art must aspire. However, unlike Plato, he does not see the relationship between art and truth as *the making of a claim* but, rather, as *a revelation*. This suggests that truth for Hegel is a preexisting generality – *the* truth – and, as we saw in Badiou's critique of the *romantic schema of art*, this truth is not a singular-ity to which every specific work of art has to make a fresh claim, but something spiritual (or, indeed, *the* Spirit) that well and truly preexists and outlasts the duration and efficacy of any work or practice of art. Also important, Hegel emphatically does not see art's crucial capacity for the satisfaction of spiritual needs as a use, but as *a vocation*. I find it a little difficult to quite understand what Hegel means by this term, and one may have to resort to properly mystical themes – *destiny*, *calling* and so on – to distinguish a vocation from a profession or from what Hegel derides, earlier in his celebrated lecture, as mere 'formal activity in accordance with given determinations'.[52] As such, one can easily anticipate Marx's materialist (and strongly atheist) misgivings about Hegel's descrip-tion of art, despite the very well-known influence that the older German thinker exerted on the young Marx. But it is important to emphasize that, despite Hegel's unwillingness to see usefulness as anything other than instrumentality (an unwillingness that he shares with the other Romantic and Idealist thinkers of his era), and despite his determination to see art as having almost a purely transcendent orientation, his connection of art's value with the satisfaction of identifiable human needs, and his emphasis on the intrinsic value of art, are evident in Marx's own approach to both art and, more generally, to the questions of labour and production.

NOTES

1. Plato, *The Republic*, trans. by H. D. P. Lee (Harmondsworth: Penguin, 1960), 375.
2. Ibid, 378.
3. Ibid.
4. Ibid, 379.
5. Ibid, 382.
6. Ibid, 384.
7. Ibid.
8. Ibid, 385.
9. Ibid.
10. Aristotle, *Poetics*, trans. Malcolm Heath (London: Penguin, 1996), 6.
11. Ibid, 7.
12. Ibid, 10.
13. Ibid, 16.
14. Ibid, 6.
15. Alain Badiou, *Handbook of Inaesthetics*, trans. Alberto Toscano (Stanford: Stanford University Press, 2005), 3.
16. Augustine of Hippo, *Confessions*, trans. R. S. Pine-Coffin (London: Penguin Books, 1961), 71.
17. Ibid, 71–72.
18. Ibid, 72.
19. Ibid, 85.
20. Ibid.
21. Ibid, 86.

22. Ibid.

23. Jean-Jacques Rousseau, *The Essential Rousseau*, trans. Lowell Bair (New York: Mentor, 1974), 224.

24. Ibid, 225.

25. Ibid, 210.

26. Ibid, 208–9.

27. Ibid, 209.

28. Ibid, 218.

29. Ibid, 207–8.

30. Ibid, 218.

31. Ibid.

32. Ibid, 219.

33. Ibid.

34. Ibid, 225–26.

35. Ibid, 225.

36. Immanuel Kant, *Critique of Judgment*, trans. James Creed Meredith (Oxford: Oxford University Press, 2008), 140.

37. Ibid, 141.

38. Ibid, 139.

39. Ibid.

40. Ibid.

41. Ibid.

42. Ibid, 135.

43. Ibid, 158.

44. Ibid, 142.

45. Georg Wilhelm Friedrich Hegel, *Introductory Lectures on Aesthetics*, trans. Bernard Bonsanquet (London: Penguin, 2004), 50.

46. Ibid, 55.

47. Ibid, 57.

48. Ibid, 35.

49. Ibid, 33.

50. Ibid, 61.

51. Ibid.

52. Ibid, 31.

2

THE INTRINSIC FREEDOM OF WRITING

Karl Marx was as much an heir to the philosophical traditions of the West as he was a heretic apropos these same traditions. His views about art are both expressed in the terms proposed by earlier philosophers – in Hegelian dialectics and in Kantian categories, most notably, but also in the Aristotelian defense of the naturalness of art – and also deeply at odds with the intentions, provenances and consequences of these terms. In keeping with the well-known – albeit, in many ways, problematic – naming of Marx's philosophy as *dialectical materialism*, one could say that Marx's theory of art reconciles a Hegelian dialectical view of art (art as an object with inherent, noninstrumental value) with his own potent take on materialism, a materialism not merely of atheism and scientific rigor, but one premised on the recognition of the foundational role of labour and production in all human phenomena.

This philosophical approach results in what is, to my mind, one of the most challenging but rewarding theories of art as yet proposed by a philosopher. It is challenging because it breaks both with our contemporary capitalist, instrumentalist views of art – that is, our view of art as, first and foremost, either a commercial or an ideological value – and also with our romantic, metaphysical notions of art which present the work as a quasi-mystical spiritual negation of the materiality of human life. According to my reading of Marx, art can be seen as the condition which comprises values that are not instrumental or reducible to the money-form and are ends in themselves, and also, at the same time, the product of the labour of real people – and definitely not the result of *inspiration* courtesy of abstract spirits, muses, cryptic unconscious urges, and the like – working in societies dominated, but never entirely possessed, by exploitative social relations and ideologies. Marx, in short, proves that art's value is a *use-value* and it is, at the same time, an *intrinsic value*.

The *genius* of Marx (a term that I am not afraid to use in a frankly Romantic fashion) can be seen in his ability to show that these two qualities of artistic value – usefulness and intrinsicality – are not contradictory but are in fact absolutely complimentary and even symbiotic: art's infinite or indefinite uses exist precisely because they spring from material human labour which, as intrinsic or *concrete* labour – prior to its reification to homogenous *abstract* labour for the purposes of exchange and commodification – seeks to produce nothing other than pure usefulness, that is, the satisfaction of humanity's most basic needs. Art, as such, is inherently useful and valuable. Furthermore, art's use and value, far from being exempt (in a Romantic, Rousseauian sense) from the sordid transactions of capitalist society, are nothing other than uses and values produced in response to the alienating ideology of this kind of society.

According to my reading of Marx's philosophy, he attempts the complex and seemingly counterintuitive task – seen as such in the context of the conventions of Marx's and perhaps our own philosophical milieus, influenced as they are by Kant, Hegel and their progeny which see any kind of use as automatically instrumentalizing – of showing that use, in the first and most concrete instance, and when seen as the outcome of natural human labour, is something akin to a *truth* that has an intrinsic value in itself (qua use-value) and only becomes a means or a utility – and a knowledge or a *technē* – later, due to the abstraction or reification of labour-power by the dominant forces in society. Since art is a product of labour – something that even Rousseau and Kant would agree upon – art too can have an *intrinsic use*; and because art's use-value is found not in the negation of the materiality of life (as Hegel might say) but in the negation of the mental or ideological dimension of the materiality of life, then, far from art's use-value being destined for suppression or obliteration in the milieu of capitalist surplus-value extraction, art retains a genuine theoretical or mental use-value which confronts the aesthetic and ideological dimensions of the capitalist world. Art can remain, with whatever level of difficulty, loyal to our drive to satisfy the very real and serious needs of our species through immanent, socially situated artistic human labour.

THE POEM OF A YOUNG PHILOSOPHER

A full account of a theory of art as *produced noninstrumental use-value* is something that emerges as part of Marx's gradual, lifelong development as one of the most important and original thinkers of the modern world. His belief in (the German Idealist concept of) art as noninstrumental value, as present in his work from very early on, is inherently conversant and unsettled by the questions of labour and ideology.

Having been excused from military service due to poor lungs (a condition which did not preclude his lifelong love of harsh, cheap cigars) and compelled by his lawyer father to abandon his passion for literature and philosophy, the eighteen-year-old Karl was sent to Berlin to study law and follow in his father's proud professional footsteps. There, much to the older Marx's dismay, the inquisitive Prussian teenager discovered the philosophy of Hegel, who had died only five years earlier in the city, where he had been the rector of the University of Berlin. With encouragement from his childhood sweetheart and fiancée, the daughter of a liberal and progressive aristocratic family, the young Marx began to read and write literature and philosophy again, and, partly to convince his father that his time – and his stipend – were not being wasted on frivolous activities, he dedicated one of his poems of 1837 to the older Marx. Titled 'Poetry', the poem can be seen as both a desperate defense of its author's chosen vocation and also a somewhat ham-fisted attempt at appeasing his father through flattery. It is also one of the first known instances of Karl Marx reflecting on the question of art.

'Poetry' is abundant with the Romantic tropes that characterize much of early nineteenth-century German and European poetry, and, perhaps needless to say, it cannot be ranked alongside work by Goethe, Heine or the like in terms of literary sophistication or poetic power. In the poem, Marx assumes the overblown, over-confident voice of a Romantic genius par excellence, claiming to have seen 'faraway skies' and to have magically reconciled the oppositions of 'pain and joy' into a 'song' thanks to the 'flames' of 'Aeolian' inspiration ignited in his breast by his father's love for him.[1] Whatever success this poem may have had in (temporarily) placating his father by paying homage to the latter's generous love for this disobedient son, it also expresses a nascent philosophy on the art of poetry. I would like to quote this short poem in its entirety – as translated into an accurate, albeit prosaic, English by S. S. Prawer, which eschews the original's *ababaa* rhyme scheme – to consider what it may auger regarding the future revolutionary thinker's philosophy:

> 'Poetry'
> Creator-like, flames streamed,
> Purling, from your breast to mine,
> High, wide, they tongued together
> And I nourished them in my breast.
> Your image stood bright, like Aeolian sound;
> Gently it covered the glow with pinions of love.
> I heard murmuring sounds, I saw a gleam,
> Faraway skies drifted along,
> Emerged to sight, sank down again,
> Sank only to rise higher still.
> When the inner struggle came to rest

I saw pain and joy concentrated in song.
Nestling against gentle forms
The soul stands rapt,
These forms grew out of me,
Your fire quickened them.
In spirit they unbend loving limbs,
They scintillate again, brightly, in their creator's bosom.[2]

Despite the profusion of Romantic clichés in the poem – and accompanying motifs such as 'soul' and 'spirit' – the poem contains some noticeably intricate and intriguing elements. The 'flames' which the semi-Promethean poet has been gifted by his father are not a source of positive, straightforward inspiration. Unlike Prometheus proper, the poet here has not in any way stolen the fire but has been given or perhaps even involuntarily subjected to it. And after the event of inspiration, the father must use his 'pinions' (*schwingen* in the original German, which could also be translated as the act of swinging or moving wings) to 'gently' cover the flames to, one can only assume, protect his son from harm. We may see this as an allegorical or secretive – or even subconscious – comment by the poet regarding his father's difficult love for his son, a love which included *pain* as well as *joy*. We may also say that, according to this text, the poem's origin or its *intrinsic purpose* – to use Kant's phrase – has something to do with the poet ('creator-like' but not initially a full creator) con/fronting something that *streams* or comes from outside of his own *breast*.

What the poet responds to, or what we might see, cautiously, as that which causes the poem, could be seen as something like an alien power that enters and interferes (*purls* and *tongues*) with the poet's own subjectivity. This *inspiration*, therefore, is not so much a kind of delightful or beautiful Romantic or Idealist moment, but a potentially darker, controlling and even frightening force that anticipates Marx's future thoughts regarding alienation and ideology. Even at such an early stage in his writing, and despite the profusion of Kantian aesthetico-perceptual signifiers of a Romantically poetic imagination – 'I heard murmuring sounds, I saw a gleam', and so forth – the actual writing or production of the poem is associated with a 'struggle' (the English translation of Marx's original *Kampf*, which is, of course, the very word used in *Klassen-kampf*, or *class struggle*). And when, finally, art emerges from the artist's *struggle* with the multifaceted *flames*, the resulting works of art are material things or *forms* that *grow out* of their maker's body and have the power – and, we might say, the value – of *scintillating brightly*. Whatever the uses of this *bright scintillation* may be, it's clear that the scintillation itself is now independent of the poem's addressee (the source of the poem's causality and its designated reader or, in a formal noncommercial sense, its consumer: Marx's father, Heinrich). In the last stanza, it's revealed that this value predates the moment of inspiration as it has been *quickened* but not conceived or created by the addressee's fire. The primary value of these products – the *bright scintillation of the gentle forms* – hence belongs to and resides intrinsically in the *bosom* of the poet who has laboured and struggled to produce them, and not in the hands of or under the *gentle loving pinions* of the poet's reader.

ART AND THE RADICAL JOURNALIST

Despite successfully completing his doctorate in philosophy at the University of Jena and writing a good deal of poetry as well as fiction and drama, and joining a group of influential intellectual proto-avant-gardists who called themselves the Young Hegelians, Marx was unable to secure a position as an academic or establish himself as a creative writer in either Berlin or Jena. The Young Hegelians were self-described radicals who aspired to participate in a German revolution modelled on (aspects of) what had happened in France in the previous generation. They were staunch atheists and secularists and despised the Prussian regime's illiberality and monarchical authoritarianism. They were Hegelians in so far as they venerated *progress* and *freedom*, but they distinguished themselves from the *old* Hegel's penchant for spirituality and Christianity. It was, at any rate, due to this group's reputation as potential troublemakers and Marx's association with them that the young would-be philosopher and poet was unable to find work in the intellectual and academic milieus of a Prussian society increasingly haunted by the specter of the French Revolution, some of whose ideals had been transported, rather aggressively, to the German-speaking world by the subject of Hegel's admiration, Napoléon Bonaparte, twenty years earlier. Napoléon had brought with his invading armies a number of distinctly modern and progressive policies – secularization and the opening of church lands to commercial activity, a secular legal code, and the emancipation of religious minorities such as Jews – and it had been after Napoléon's defeat three years before Karl Marx's birth that Karl's Jewish father had had to convert to Lutheranism – and hence change his name from Herschel to Heinrich – to remain registered as a lawyer in the reactionary, antisemitic aftermath of the brief French rule over parts of Prussia.

Upon returning to his native Rhineland in 1841 at the age of twenty-three, the somewhat dejected Karl may have missed the boisterous, heady social circles of Berlin, but he would have found no shortage of sympathy for reform and radicalism among his fellow Rhinelanders. His own father, despite his seemingly traditional desire to see his son take up a good, respectable upper-middle-class profession, had remained a passionate supporter of the liberal aspects of the French Revolution and its Napoleonic sequel. Marx's fiancée Johanna 'Jenny' von Westphalen's father was a nobleman and a Prussian government official who had first entered politics under French rule and had continued to openly harbor reformist and radical ideals during the reactionary restoration of absolutist Prussian sovereignty. It was in part due to his influence that his friend Heinrich's erudite and strong-headed son, Karl, was employed to edit the liberal, antiauthoritarian newspaper *Rheinische Zeitung* to advance the agendas of the progressive Prussian intellectuals of this era. And it is in an editorial published in this newspaper in 1842, in response to the debate about press freedom, that we find Marx starting to sketch a thesis apropos art, its nature, and its value.

Considering the newspaper's openly liberal agenda and its progressive readership, it should not surprise us that the former poet
and now increasingly radical journalist champions free speech,
one of the key ideals of the highly Enlightened German Idealists.
But the manner of Marx's early discourse, if not its intentions,
already hints at the thinker's emerging understanding of both the
dynamics of capitalism and the role of the writer as a producer or a
worker, themes that are almost entirely absent from the liberal
discourses of Marx's immediate social and intellectual milieu. (Although it should be noted that Marx's aristocratic future father-in-
law had already introduced him to the writings of early French
socialists.) Marx's argument may at first appear very much like a
Hegelian celebration of the value of writing as something *higher*
than that of any manual metier; but it is also evident that Marx
recognizes that this evaluation is not based on a concrete difference between the modes of mental (e.g., artistic and literary) as
opposed to physical production, but dependent on an abstract
quasi-religious *belief* in the superiority of art's intrinsic value, and
hence in the categorical need for the maintenance of press freedom. The young liberal Marx is clearly a believer in the absolute
generality and essentiality of freedom – 'freedom of trade, freedom of property, of conscience, of the press, of the courts, are all
species of the same genus, of *freedom without any specific
name*'³ – and attempts to defend press freedom by showing the
absurdity of the Prussian rulers' fondness for, on the one hand,
accepting free trade and, on the other, suppressing free speech:

> One could also [put the question of freedom] the other way
> round and call freedom of trade merely *a variety of freedom of
> the press*. Do craftsmen work only with hands and legs and not
> with the brain as well? Is the language of words the only lan-
> guage of thought? Is not the language of the mechanic through
> the steam-engine easily perceptible to my ear, is not the lan-
> guage of the bed manufacturer very obvious to my back, that of
> the cook comprehensible to my stomach? Is it not a contradic-
> tion that all these varieties of freedom of the press are permit-

ted, the sole exception being the one that speaks to my intellect through the medium of the printer's ink?[4]

Marx's attempt to equate a writer's freedom to do his or her job with another producer's freedom to do likewise, with the aim of showing the irrationality of suppressing a writer's freedom through censorship, may be seen as a mostly rhetorical and perhaps far-fetched device used for proving an argument. But one must not gloss over the deeply non-Hegelian implications of Marx's approach. As mentioned before, key to Hegel's view that art possesses, first and foremost, a spiritual value is the assumption that art is not *formal or mechanical activity in accordance with given determinations*. But if as Marx has argued, the engine operator, the bedmaker and the chef also produce aesthetico-linguistic objects, then does it not follow that the writer too produces *useful* objects à la the bedmaker and the chef? If, as Marx would have it, manual workers do not 'work only with hands and legs and . . . with the brain as well', then can't it also be said that writers and mental workers do not only work with the brain but use hands and legs as well? Is there not a potential here for dissolving the vaunted Kantian distinction between *fine* and *mechanical* arts?

In the same article, Marx argues passionately against the Prussian government censors' hypothetical division of authors into *authorized* and *unauthorized* writers, with the aim of instituting a practice according to which only an author with official knowledge or authority regarding a contentious political topic – who, needless to say, would be a member of or associated with the Prussian political class – would be invited (or allowed) to write on that topic. Marx uses an intensely egalitarian argument against this proposal, by asserting that the 'special external signs' of authority and expertise are, in fact, the 'means of external privilege' and that the press – which, according to the brazenly idealistic young journalist, 'knows no respect for persons, but only respect for intelligence' – must be open to publishing works by all people on all topics, because 'just as everyone learns to read and write, so everyone must have the right to read and write'.[5] In a specifically Hege-

lian rhetorical spirit – which, as we have seen, would see the satisfaction of *spiritual needs* as art's highest aim – Marx addresses the
Prussian government officials and tells them that if he (as a nonex-
pert and a nonauthorized writer) loses the right to publish his
writing then he cannot be 'a spiritual force for others' and, therefore, he 'has no right to be a spiritual force for myself'. He accuses,
in other words, the censorious government of stunting his own
spiritual development and, by so doing, harming the spirituality,
faith, morals and even civic values of the Kingdom, which is the
very thing the censors are supposed to be protecting.

Based on this analysis, it can be said that, at this part of his
article, the young Marx is putting egalitarianism at the service of a
liberalism that equates freedom with a categorical benefit and
scorns any imposition against it. However, as Marx develops his
counterargument apropos the discourse of *authorized* and *unauthorized* writerly identities, he amplifies the implication of his belief in the universal capacity to read and write, and, by traversing
the demand for the right to free speech, he comes dangerously
close to affronting one of the tenets of both Romantic and Idealist
philosophies of art, the figure of the exceptional artistic genius.
Despite their differences in describing the figure of the genius,
Romantics and Idealists (including Hegel) subscribe to the figure's
crucial and liberating attributes. For Hegel, for example, the genius *frees* the work of art from the finitude of its *mechanical* nature
by making it (not altogether unconsciously, as a particular kind of
Romantic might have it) an object of the Spirit via her or his
artistic imagination. Admittedly, it is not Marx's intention to
undermine the (conceptually) necessary figure of a *divinely imaginative* artistic genius and its liberal consequences, and yet, in arguing that *authorized* mediocrity – of the professional, academic
kind, at the service of the authoritarian states – is quite useless and
has not served the interests of the German civilization, he (perhaps inadvertently) also criticizes the antiegalitarian position of
the *unauthorized* genius. He writes:

If the German looks back on his history, he will find one of the main reasons for his slow political development, as also for the wretched state of literature prior to *Lessing*, in the existence of *'authorised writers'*. The learned men by profession, guild or privilege, the doctors and others, the colourless university writers of the seventeenth and eighteenth centuries, with their stiff pigtails and their distinguished pedantry and their petty hairsplitting dissertations, interposed themselves between the people and the mind, between life and science, between freedom and mankind. It was the unauthorised writers who created our literature. *Gottsched* and Lessing – there you have the choice between an 'authorised' and 'unauthorized' writer![6]

The differentiation between the universally loathed and lampooned pedant and careerist Johann Gottsched and the internationally lauded figurehead of the German Enlightenment, Gotthold Lessing – each as a representative of a type of writer who would or would not be favored by the Prussian government's proposed policy on press freedom – is made to mock the philistinism of the Prussian officials and to portray them as actual opponents of the Kingdom's cultural interests. Here, Gottssched stands for a false genius, a *colourless* pretender who only has the *privilege* of an important academic *profession*. (Note the typical Idealist dismissal of a mere *profession* as opposed to a more exulted *vocation*.) The influential playwright and philosopher Lessing, on the other hand, is a true genius, one of the *creators of German literature*, whose famous plays, one can safely assume, did not lack *colour*, vibrancy, and so on. And yet, is the certifiably brilliant Lessing too not a figure *interposed between the people and the mind, between life and science, between freedom and humankind*? Would a truly empowered and emancipated people – so many of whom, as Marx has already told us, can read and write – not be the real creators of their own literature, in no need for divinely imaginative writers to bring freedom to their minds? Would it not be humankind itself – and neither the laughable state-sanctioned fraud nor the authentic Enlightened genius – that would be the true unauthorized author of their own literature and lives?

Perhaps aware of the deeply anti-Idealist direction that his arguments have taken, the young Hegelian Marx asserts, immediately after the first of the above-quoted passages, a belief in 'the nobility of [the] nature' of journalism and the press, and warns against the press 'degrad[ing] itself to the level of trade'.[7] However, even here, the innately anti-elitist Marx does not shy away from stating that this degradation is not the consequence of a *high* spiritual mental activity being brought down to the level of *low* physical production – the degradation occurs when mental activity is reduced to a merely *commercial* activity. Marx is already breaking with the commonly accepted teleology of commodity-value production, the dominant economic aspiration of the same intellectuals and progressives with whom he has identified thus far in his life, when he writes: 'The writer, of course, must earn in order to be able to live and write, but he must by no means live and write to earn'.[8] He repeats – and clearly sincerely agrees with – the Hegelian injunction against instrumentalization, but he is also suspicious that the specifically Hegelian appraisal of the intrinsic value of art may be akin to a religious piety:

> The writer does not at all look on his work as a *means*. It is an *end in itself*, it is so little a means for him himself and others that, if need be, he sacrifices *his* existence to *its* existence. He is, in another way, like the preacher of religion who adopts the principle: 'Obey God rather than man', including under man himself with his human needs and desires. On the other hand, what if a tailor from whom I had ordered a Parisian frock-coat were to come and bring me a Roman toga on the grounds that it was more in keeping with the eternal law of beauty![9]

There is much that can be said about the above passage, and one may note the young Marx's self-identification as a bourgeois consumer (of a Parisian frock-coat, of all things) prior to his losing his handsomely paid job as a journalist with the suppression of *Rheinische Zeitung* by Prussian government censors in 1843 due to the publication of an article critical of Russian monarchy. It is important to note, in the context of our discussion about art and value, that for Marx, while art may have an intrinsic value similar to a religious vocation, it lacks an actual use only insofar as it can't be *ordered* from a producer. The problem with the Roman toga is not only that it has artistic pretentions beyond the tangible instrumental value of a modern coat, but that in the process of a consumer's purchasing of a product from a producer, *the eternal law of beauty* has been reified and reduced to an object with only an exchange-value. In an echo of Rousseau's contempt for luxury and his own burgeoning understanding of commodification, Marx is starting to become aware of the negative instrumentalizing consequences of the new bourgeois economic modes of production and consumption, an observation that is repeated, more explicitly, in his longest work of journalism, 'On the Jewish Question', written immediately after the closure of *Rheinische Zeitung*.

Once again jobless, and now married to Jenny, Marx was compelled to move to France to both evade further harassment by Prussian authorities and help Young Hegelian radicals in exile with founding a new periodical called *Deutsch–Französische Jahrbücher*, to be published in Paris and illegally smuggled into Prussia. In Paris, while rapidly spending whatever money he and Jenny had on a lavish honeymoon, Marx was deeply affected by the social atmosphere of the *cradle of revolution*. He became more conversant with and involved in socialism and communism. It is during this period, with his growing preoccupation with socioeconomic matters – and under the influence of a particular strand of French socialism that equates capitalism with accumulation of private property – that he wrote 'On the Jewish Question' in response to an article by another Young Hegelian, Bruno Bauer, who had claimed that Jewish emancipation should not be a priority for Prussian radicals.

Marx, observing that in much of Europe and European history Judaism and capitalism have become conceptually intertwined due to socioeconomic dynamics (a view which, as we have seen, is retained by Marx and is repeated, more than twenty years later, in the motif of the interstice in *Capital, Volume One*), aims to show that, contrary to Bauer, the emancipation of Jews is of foremost importance. By giving the Jews the same rights as other Prussian citizens, Jews will be liberated from the binds of a jaundiced and phantasmagoric or *'chimerical'*[10] Judaism of the European imagination – which he calls 'the Judaism of civil society'[11] – which is, according to Marx, the religion of bourgeois greed and egoism itself. Such an emancipation would presage and precipitate the emancipation of the entire society from bourgeois religion of *'practical interest'* and *'self-interest'* whose 'god' is nothing other than *'money'*.[12] He writes:

> Money is the jealous god of Israel before whom no other god may stand. Money debases all the gods of mankind and turns them into commodities. Money is the universal and self-constituted *value* of all things. It has therefore deprived the entire world – both the world of man and of nature – of its specific value. Money is the estranged essence of man's work and existence; this alien essence dominates him and he worships it.[13]

I will consider the question of the *estranged alien essence* that has come to dominate modern humans – and the question of the extent and finality of this domination – in some detail in a chapter of its own (chapter 5) as it is central to Marx's philosophy of art. For now, it should be noted that the pejorative reference to Israel in this passage and to Judaism elsewhere in 'On the Jewish Question' should not be seen as antisemitic because, as already mentioned, here Marx is dealing exclusively with the image of Judaism constructed by the European Christian mind; what he is commenting on is 'not the *sabbath Jews'*, but the Jews as seen through 'the religious eye of the Christian'.[14] Nor does he accuse his opponent, Bauer, of antisemitism – although such an accusation may be indirectly implied by Marx's essay – but instead criticizes him for not being sufficiently opposed to *the god of money*. It is clear that, unlike many other Young Hegelian radicals, Marx is becoming increasingly less interested in the topics of free speech and secularism and more concerned with poverty and economic inequality.

The crucial differentiation between two kinds of value – between money, on the one hand, and the *specific value* of things prior to the imposition of a bourgeois monetary value system, on the other – in the above-quoted passage indicates Marx's readings in economic theory, even prior to his meeting and the commencement of his pivotal lifelong collaboration with the exceptionally insightful and enthusiastic young fellow-German labour theorist, Friedrich Engels.

Here, Marx follows on and develops the theme of art's degradation from his earlier journalism. He writes that while in a traditional religion – the bane of many a liberal, atheist progressive's existence – there 'is present in an abstract form' a 'contempt for theory, for art', this abstract *contempt* becomes an '*actual* and *conscious* standpoint' in the bourgeois 'man of money'.[15] As an analogy and an example of the actualization of an abstract disdain, he notes how 'the relation between man and woman' has become a 'commercial object', as a result of which 'woman is put on the market'.[16] Woman is objectified not simply because of man's abstract contempt for her as an end in herself – misogyny – but because, under the bourgeois dominance of *man of money*, she (like many male humans, too) has become a means to an end. Under capitalism, a woman no longer possesses her own *intrinsic* or specific value – or what she is to herself – but becomes an instrument for the accumulation of more capital. However, while a woman's *debasement* and her *being turned into a commodity* in, for example, the modern sex industry can be quite visible and graphic – the extent of which in mid-nineteenth-century Paris must have startled the young Prussian intellectual – the similarly *actual* and *conscious* perversion of art under the bourgeoisie takes a far less visible form, and it became one of the major concerns of Marx's next, and first book-length, work.

NOTES

1. Marx, 'Poetry', trans. S. S. Prawer, quoted in S. S. Prawer, *Karl Marx and World Literature* (Oxford: Oxford University Press, 1978), 5.

2. Ibid.

3. Marx, 'On Freedom of the Press', *Marxist Internet Archive*, accessed 27 July 2017, https://www.marxists.org/archive/marx/works/1842/free-press/index.htm.

4. Ibid.

5. Ibid.

6. Ibid.

7. Ibid.

8. Ibid.

9. Ibid.

10. Marx, *Early Writings*, trans. Rodney Livingstone and Gregor Benton (London: Penguin, 1992), 239.

11. Ibid, 238.

12. Ibid, 239.

13. Ibid.

14. Ibid, 236.

15. Ibid, 239.

16. Ibid.

3

ART, SPECULATION AND IDEOLOGY

THE ABJECT ART OF THE BOURGEOISIE

It was almost immediately after publishing 'On the Jewish Question', still in a relatively early stage of his intellectual development, that Marx openly, and with open hostility, rejected the Hegelian Idealism of his youth and started to propose an explicitly materialist philosophy that is trenchantly opposed to bourgeois liberalism. In his first books and first major collaborations with Engels, *The Holy Family* (1844) and *The German Ideology* (1845), Marx forcefully attacks many of the Young Hegelian intellectuals whom he had until recently viewed as comrades, including Bauer, Max Stirner and their disciples, such as a Prussian soldier called Franz Zychlin von Zychlinski who, under the pseudonym Szeliga, had written a rather effusive appreciation of a popular French novel of the period by Eugène Sue.

In some of his most extensive writings on literature, in the fifth and eighth chapters of *The Holy Family*, Marx lambasts what he sees as the Hegelians' untenably speculative and abstract – in short, nonmaterialist – understanding of art and literature, by noting that Szeliga's view of the literary work depends upon a belief that the work is a manifestation of the theme of *mystery*. This perspective is not only due to the title of Sue's novel – *The Myster-*

ies of Paris – but also due to the Hegelian view of art as *spiritual revelation*. As quoted by Marx in *The Holy Family*, a garish Parisian ballroom scene in the novel is interpreted by Szeliga as 'the miracle of the divine presence in the breast of man, especially when beauty and grace uphold the conviction that we are in the immediate proximity of ideals'.[1] Marx is quick to mock Szeliga's rather fanciful reading – and calls the Hegelian an 'inexperienced, credulous *Critical country parson*'![2] – but, despite the scathing tone of Marx's attacks on his former fellow-Hegelians, this condemnation is not personal and is in fact based on a patiently developed argument against some of the key assumptions of the Hegelian philosophy or what Marx calls '*speculative Hegelian construction*'.[3]

According to Marx, key elements of the Hegelian philosophy – among which we may include Hegel's belief in the nonutilitarian value of art qua the satisfaction of a spiritual need – are based on a system of abstraction or speculation that, in trying to understand the world and its profane realities, commits the error of imposing an *essential* configuration over *substantial* corporeality. The practitioner of such a philosophy, having concocted a purely abstract mental image or ideal from encounters with the tangible components of the world – having posited 'the general idea "Fruit"', for example, as 'the *true* essence of the pear, the apple, etc.'[4] – is then forced to move in 'a speculative, mystical fashion'[5] in accounting for the concrete and diverse actualities of the world. Such thinkers come to think that fruits 'have a higher mystic significance, which are grown out of the ether of your brain and not out of the material earth'.[6] And it is this systemic ignorance of the material which marks the Hegelian literary critic Szeliga as *credulous* and *inexperienced*. Szeliga has imposed his own essential trope or general idea of mystery on the topics and textual actualities of the novel, mistaking *The Mysteries of Paris* for a mystical and altogether uplifting account of man's moral and spiritual journey, instead of seeing it, as Marx does, as an account of an aristocratic protagonist's duplicitous and self-serving trickery and his ability or privilege to disguise himself as a commoner and, by so doing, gain 'entry into the lower sections of society' so that he can later claim 'how extraordinarily interesting he finds himself in the various situations'.[7]

Marx, in short, sees ruling class vanity and egoism in the discourse of a literary work that the high-minded, progressive Hegelians find ethical or spiritual. It would be tempting to see Marx's shift of focus away from the liberal preoccupations of the German progressives towards socialist concerns with class as occasioned by his move to the radical milieu of French activism and also his growing awareness and study of English economic theory. It would be equally convenient to see Marx's irreversible move in a socialist direction in mid-1840s as a consequence of the revolutionary zeitgeist which anticipated the 1848 European revolutions; political conflicts which pitted not only the bourgeois liberals against the conservative nobility, but also brought the bourgeoisie in direct conflict with the poor and the proletariat. However, Marx's own claim would be that, irrespective of one's political affiliations – his increasingly uncompromising socialism versus the Hegelians' increasingly commonplace liberalism – there is something inherently untenable and irrational about the Hegelian view of art qua something that has a noninstrumental albeit moral or spiritual value. It replaces what it perceives as the practical or mechanical instrumentalization of things in the real 'world system' (e.g., art as something with a finite educational or cathartic utility) with an equally – and perhaps even more – instrumentalized conception of things as the 'fantastic' concrete materializations of immaterial moral, ideal or spiritual attributes.[8] The Hegelian view of art, therefore, results in 'distortion and *senseless abstraction* of reality'.[9]

Furthermore, Marx is not only critical of critics who have sought to find authorization for their own ideals in literary works; he also finds in the novel itself a literary philosophy and a poetics every bit as abstract and idealizing as the distorted thought of its Hegelian admirer. He describes Sue, the author of the novel, as acting against the *real* or *human* interests and properties of his characters – and therefore Marx attributes to the fictional characters elements of agency and subjectivity autonomous to the desires of their fiction-writing creator – by imposing the novelist's own authorial perspective on the characters' internal motivations and external actions. Sue, according to Marx, is 'the great moralist' who 'satisfies his monkish, bestial lust'[10] by humiliating and punishing the characters who fall short of his ideals, such as a criminal working-class man who is physically tortured, blinded and reduced to *'canine* devotion'[11] before the novel's upper-class protagonist. Marx detects in Sue's characterization of a young working-class woman or *grisette* a subtler albeit more telling attempt by the author to subject a female character from one class to the sexual mores of the women of another – the author's own – higher class:

> Sue describes in her the lovely human character of the Paris girl of the people. Only his devotedness to the bourgeoisie and his own personal love of exaggeration made him idealize Grisette *morally.* He could not refrain from smoothing down the asperities of her situation in life and her character, to be precise, her disdain for the form of marriage, her naïve attachment to the young *student* or the *worker.* It is precisely in that attachment that she constitutes a really human contrast to the hypocritical, narrow-hearted, self-seeking wife of the bourgeois, to the whole circle of the bourgeoisie, that it, to the official circle.[12]

Whereas in many other parts of the novel Sue has succeeded in submitting the characters to his class ideals and their moral dimension – by showing, for example, that as the chastised and blinded former criminal 'become a *"moral being"*, he has also adopted the gait and demeanour of the *petty bourgeois*'[13] – the free-spirited young Parisian woman seems to have retained some of her (stereotypical) non-middle-class *grisette* qualities, such as her *lovely human character* and her *naïve* sexual attraction to men of her own class. The novelist, nevertheless, has tried to *smooth down* this roughness by presenting her refusal to be courted or romanced as a chaste and moral disavowal of improper sexual behavior, and not as a rejection of the novel's cherished moral motif of marriage which is, of course, also one of the tenets of bourgeois social values and amorous ideals.

In *The Holy Family*, Marx is never less than emphatic that the subject of his criticism is not only the pre- or protobourgeois mindset of the Hegelian enthusiast of *The Mysteries of Paris*, but also the novel's own thoroughly bourgeois literary qualities which express the dominant ideals of its world. As he notes apropos the novel's central character Rudolph's plan to reform the society, Rudolph's 'theory is nothing but the theory of the society of to-day'.[14]

One such theory is the notion of charity or philanthropy which, according to Marx's lacerating reading of the novel, is nothing other than a class ideal. By closely analysing a scene in the novel in which the do-gooding, albeit wily, Rudolph entices an initially unwilling and very wealthy Frenchwoman to donate money to 'poor Poles' by tempting her with the prospect of an opulent and decadent charity gala – and by so doing crassly utilizing or instrumentalizing her basic '*human impulses*', something that the novel's Hegelian aficionado, despite the supposed injunction against instrumentalization, does not at all mind doing, as this utilization supposedly serves a *higher* purpose, that is, helping those *poor Poles* – Marx shows that here the poor people's 'misery is exploited consciously to procure' for the rich the opportunity to both have glamorous balls and feel *good* (i.e., moral and virtuous) while doing so.[15] Marx writes: 'Rudolph has thereby unconsciously expressed the mystery that was revealed long ago that human misery itself, infinite abjectness which is obliged to receive alms, must serve as a *plaything* to the aristocracy of the money and education to satisfy their self-love, tickle their arrogance and amuse them'.[16]

Here and in the final sections of his extensive commentary on *The Mysteries of Paris*, Marx is arguing that the novelist, the novel's narrator and protagonist, and the novel's admirers are not only advancing a philosophically flawed and unbearably abstract and unreliable perspective, but that this perspective is bound up with the self-satisfying ideals and moral interests of the ascending socioeconomic class of *the aristocracy of the money and education*, that is, the industrial and commercial bourgeoisie, the class fast displacing the old aristocracy of land and titles as the dominant political and cultural group in all Western European societies. According to Marx, the novel borders on out-and-out political propaganda by advocating, however *unconsciously* on the part of its author or main characters, a 'political-economic' agenda for the modern society, according to which '*hereditary* and *private ownership* are and *must* be inviolable and sacred' and the task of the state is to reach a compromise between '*capital and labour*' so that the workers will continue to work and generate capital for the owners of industries '*without* prejudice to the *fortune of the rich*'; to fabricate '*links* of sympathy between these *two classes* and thus guarantee calm in the state *for ever*'.[17] As Western Europe moved closer to a period of revolutionary social upheaval, Marx found in *The Mysteries of Paris* and its German admirers, the working of the modern ruling-class, antirevolutionary *ideology*.

Marx's sensational discovery of modern ideology in *The German Ideology*, which, as is well known, has been said to mark his *epistemological break* with Hegelian philosophy, has been too extensively written about by the recent proponents of Western Marxism to require explanation here.[18] For the purposes of our mapping and investigation of Marx's philosophy of art, it is important to point out that in *The German Ideology*, alongside the continuation of his philosophical disparagement of individual Hegelians, Marx and Engels are now proposing an alternative and economic-materialist theory of historical progress, one which accounts not only for why liberal intellectuals make the laughable and mistaken assumptions lampooned in *The Holy Family*, but also strives to locate the material origins and social locality of the class for which these intellectuals speak. Marx and Engels' seminal, dramatic identification of the modern, upper middle classes or the bourgeoisie as the ruling class of the modern world, and the shift of the target of the revolutionaries' ire from conservative *ancien régime* nobility and clergy towards the industrial and financial bourgeoisie, is articulated both in a class theory, founded on an analysis of the modes and relations of physical and monetized production (such as manufacture, property ownership, agriculture, etc.) and also in a theory of the modes and relations of *mental and ideological production* which includes, among other things, what could be seen as an understanding of art as something related to ruling class ideology.

Indeed, it would not be difficult to say that, based on a somewhat superficial reading of *The German Ideology*, Marx, who once had rather exultant things to say about the arts – who, as a young would-be Romantic poet, had claimed that one should live only to write and that one should be ready to forfeit one's existence for art – is now, as a would-be internationalist revolutionary who will soon be drawn in to the world of real, violent antigovernmental agitation and political activity, has come to question the value and the usefulness of art. If, as he and Engels now famously claim, 'the ideas of ruling class are in every epoch the ruling ideas: i.e., the class which is the ruling *material* force of society is at the same time its ruling *intellectual* force',[19] then can't it be said that artistic production, as a species of intellectual production, is determined or at least enlisted by ruling class forces, and that it has no real or serious intrinsic value for a position opposed to the power of the ruling class? In support of such a view – which more than brings to mind Plato's injunction against the arts – we may cite Marx and Engels' continued preoccupation with the hapless Hegelians in *The German Ideology*. Here, Marx and Engels ridicule the 'lofty moral postulate'[20] of one of the chief Hegelian public intellectuals, Max Stirner, for whom 'creative activity is . . . only a paraphrase of speculative reflection or pure essence'.[21] Is *creative activity* as such not the problem, then, if it is so easily coopted in the faulty speculative, moralist enterprise of a protobourgeois intellectual? And does Marx and Engels's view, further on in the book, that it is the former aristocratic ruling classes' 'direct, naïve outlook on life which finds expression in memoirs, poems, novels, etc.',[22] not an unambiguous dismissal of so many genres of literature as mere *expressions* of a ruling class ideology?

In Marx's oeuvre, there is no shortage of remarks which seemingly equate art with the ruling classes and their ideology. In a fragment of an incomplete manuscript written in Paris at around the same time as *The German Ideology*, Marx depicts poetry as an alibi or a conceptual tool used by the former ruling class of the feudal nobility in the ideological standoff with the new ruling class of the capitalist bourgeoisie. The agrarian aristocrat 'lays stress on the noble lineage of his property, on feudal mementos, reminiscences, the poetry of recollection' and accuses the bourgeois of lacking 'honour, principles, poetry'.[23] And while the weakened nobles try to cling, rather desperately, to their ideological prominence by resorting to (a conceptually instrumentalized view of) the oldest and most venerated of the literary forms, the agile and ascending capitalists include more recent artistic forms in their arsenal of ideological weapons. In another fragment from the same period of writing, Marx notes that the nineteenth-century 'moral ideal' of 'the *ascetic* but *productive* slave' – a modern worker or a *wage slave* who is compelled to work hard for the (bourgeois) boss to earn more and yet, at the same time, is also made to feel guilty about spending her or his earnings on genuinely pleasurable or humanizing pursuits – finds 'ready-made an abject *art* in which to clothe this its pet idea: they [the bourgeoisie] have presented it, bathed in sentimentality, on the stage'.[24] So modern realist drama is not only as *sentimental* as old poetry, but it is also equally *abject* or servile to ideological objectives of a ruling class.

A more forceful example of the bourgeois assimilation of art and ideology may be found in an arresting and acerbic passage from a book written almost thirty years later, Marx's powerful account of the Paris Commune, *The Civil War in France*. Here Marx notes that, during the brief rule of the workers in Paris and the battles between the Communards and the French government forces, the affluent Parisian bourgeoisie – *francs-fileurs* or absconders – abandoned much of the city to hide from 'the real Paris', away from the embattled proletarian revolutionaries and the besieged working-class suburbs. Thus, what the bourgeoise saw of the historic event they saw only through an ideological lens which was, simultaneously, an artistic prism, characterized with ennui, decadence and spleen à la Baudelaire, in a phantom Paris, the Paris of the *francs-fileurs*, the Paris of the Boulevards, male and female – the rich, the capitalist, the gilded, the idle Paris, now thronging with its lackeys, its black-legs, its literary *bôhème*, and its cocottes at Versailles, Saint-Denis, Rueil, and Saint-Germain; considering the civil war but an agreeable diversion, eyeing the battle going on through tele-scopes, counting the rounds of cannon, and swearing by their own honour and that of their prostitutes, that the performance was far better got up than it used to be at Porte St. Martin. The men who fell were really dead; the cries of the wounded were cries in good earnest; and, besides, the whole thing was so intensely historical.[25]

Here, as in 'On the Jewish Question', the sexual objectification of women and the ideological objectification of art correspond. And while, as with prostitution, the degradation of art is indeed a very old profession – as seen in the exploitation of poetry by the aristocrats of the old regimes, for example – the new capitalist world has invented and propagated a new, more aesthetically am-bitious consciousness that subordinates art to ideology much more effectively. The passion for verisimilitude, for example, and the bourgeois spectator's *intense* desire to see the real men and wom-en dying in the battles and skirmishes of the civil war of 1871 as believable and *earnest* actors in a *historical* show or *performance* similar to the plays performed at the Porte St. Martin theatre does not (simply) mark the bourgeois consumers as macabre, deluded or cynical. According to this darkly satirical account, a modern artistic appreciation – for high-tech, believable stage productions, for literary bohemianism and avant-gardism, and so on – belongs to the very milieu of the bourgeois capitalists and their abject *lackeys*, and provides this *phantom* world with the means – the *telescope* – for looking at the *real* world, and, by so doing, distort-ing, falsifying and objectifying it.

Therefore, should art not be condemned or at least dismissed in our struggles for justice and equality? And should we be sur-prised to find, upon returning to the Marx of *The German Ideolo-gy*, that he and Engels belittle the other German socialists of their era as facile and politically futile members of a 'social literary movement that has come into being without any real party interests', as mere 'literary men' who, when seen from a revolutionary perspective, are either 'quacks' or 'sterile and broken-down'.[26] No wonder, then, that almost ten years later, in one of his essays on French politics – *The Eighteenth Brumaire of Louis-Napoléon* – Marx dismisses the antirevolutionary Social Democratic members of the French National Assembly, who wished to see 'class struggle avoided', as 'the "literary" representatives' of the petty bourgeoisie.[27]

TOWARDS A MATERIALIST ART

It would be a major mistake, however, to see the maturing and politically radicalized Marx as an opponent of art. It is not art as such that he attacks in his writings from the mid-1840s onwards, but art's crass ideological instrumentalizations at the services of the bourgeoisie. When denouncing the Young Hegelians, Marx is not disparaging all belief in the power of art, but reproving his former friends for their inability to offer a genuinely noninstrumental theory of artistic value. While Marx, by the mid-1840s, has come to reject the fanciful, Idealist view of art, he has not come to do so as a political militant suspicious of the arts and their potential guilt of collusion with repressive ideologies. He has instead developed, in concert with his attacks on liberalism and his exposition of bourgeois liberals' material economic interests, a powerful theory of labour and production, and he does not criticize the proponents of *creative activity* per se but criticizes those who see creative activity as a metaphysical, mystical enterprise and not as socially situated *laboured* production.

In *The German Ideology*, Marx and Engels dismiss as 'nonsense' Stirner's belief that one can be a *born poet* or a *born musician* not because Marx thinks that one cannot be a great poet – or that one cannot develop from the time of birth qualities, skills and values that could constitute the art of poetry – but because of the blatant logical inconsistency in the Hegelian's argument which tries to prove

> on the one hand, that a born poet, etc., *remains* what he *is* from birth – namely a poet, etc.; and, on the other hand, that the born poet, etc., in so far as he *becomes*, develops, may 'owing to unfavourable circumstances', not become what *he could become*. His example, therefore, on the one hand, proves nothing at all and, on the other hand, proves the opposite of what it was intended to prove.[28]

Against a naïve, excessively Romantic belief in natural artistic genius and a negative view of the world as an obstacle to the becoming of natural artistic genius, Marx argues that the world is the material context for artistic development, and the material circumstances of the world, instead of being seen as either positive or negative apropos the development of talent, should be seen as the basic conditions for the existence of all phenomena associated with the arts and human creativity, including talent. This theory of talent is clearly conversant with economic theory, as explicated two years after *The German Ideology*, in *The Poverty of Philosophy*, Marx's 1847 polemic against another former ally – the French anarchist ideologue Pierre-Joseph Proudhon – in which Marx approvingly quotes the eighteenth-century Scottish economist Adam Smith's view that perceived 'differences in natural talents in different men' are 'the *effect* of the division of labour'.[29]

In their unrelenting attack on Max Stirner in *The German Ideology*, Marx and Engels elaborate on a materialist view of art contra Stirner and other German Idealists whose materialism stopped at denouncing old feudal Judeo-Christian religions but did not take into consideration the materiality of the modes, means and divisions of economic production and development – as well as their moral, ideological, aesthetic and, in their own modern atheistic ways, profoundly superstitious or speculative dimensions – under contemporary capitalism. Stirner, in keeping with common Romantic obsessions with artistic originality and

exceptionality, adheres to the strict Kantian differentiation between *fine* and *mechanical* arts. He believes that while certain
types of labour – 'only such work as can be done for us by others,
such as cattle-slaughtering, ploughing, etc.' – can be organized
(and industrialized and exploited by capitalists for profit), artistic
work remains *unique* and *egoistical* as it can be carried out solely
by a specific human ego, that is, a particular artist – because,
according to Stirner, 'No one can do Raphael's work for him' – and
the arts therefore fall outside of the sphere of material or economic conditions.[30] After noting that Stirner is factually wrong – because 'Raphael himself "completed" only an insignificant part of
his own frescoes'[31] – Marx and Engels explain that, far from being
exempt from material conditions such as the division of labour,
Raphael's art is very much an exemplar of these material conditions, such as the division between the master or leader of the
artistic project and the team of artists who executed the work.

Against Stirner's 'bureaucratic fantasies', the teams of appren-
tices and assistants who produced the bulk of Raphael's Vatican
frescoes were not 'machine labor', but seen by their immediate
organizers – for example, Raphael himself who assessed their abil-
ities and employed them – as humans in 'whom there is a potential
Raphael'.[32] This transformation of 'not directly productive' labour
into 'directly productive labour'[33] is precisely one of the hallmarks
of a particular phase of socioeconomic development during the
Italian Renaissance, and it is, far from being unique or egoistical,
in fact quite general and social. Marx and Engels write that Stirner

> imagines that Raphael produced his pictures independently of
> the division of labour that existed in Rome at the time. If he
> were to compare Raphael with Leonardo da Vinci and Titian,
> he would see how greatly Raphael's works of art depended on
> the flourishing of Rome at that time, which occurred under
> Florentine influence, while the works of Leonardo depended
> on the state of things in Florence, and the works of Titian, at a
> later period, depended on the totally different development of
> Venice. Raphael as much as any other artist was determined by

the technical advances in art made before him, by the organisation of society and the division of labour in his locality, and,
finally, by the division of labour in all the countries with which
his locality had intercourse. [34]

And it is not only the specific case of Raphael's larger projects,
but artistic practices in their generality, which can be used to
illustrate the paradigm of the division of labour. Years later, in
Capital, Volume One, Marx uses an artistic, musical example to
portray the emergence of the necessity for division of labour or a
separation between *conductors* and *players* as the consequence of
the need for syncretized cooperation between workers. He writes:

> All combined labour on a large scale requires, more or less, a
> directing authority, in order to secure the harmonious working
> of the individual activities, and to perform the general func-
> tions that have their origin in the action of the combined or-
> ganism, as distinguished from the action of separate organs. A
> single violin player is his own conductor; an orchestra requires
> a separate one. [35]

And, as in *Capital, Volume One*, the materialist or socioeconomic view of art in *The German Ideology* is also oriented towards
a radical, emancipatory direction – here Marx and Engels strive to
undermine and, in fact, obliterate 'the exclusive concentration of
artistic talent in particular individuals, and its suppression in the
broad mass which is bound up with this'. [36] Against what I noted
earlier as the possibility of reading Marx's critique of art's confla-
tion with ideology as a denunciation of art, it should now be noted
that art has a value of its own, irrespective of its ideological coop-
tion, since countering the *suppression* of *artistic talents* in *the
broad masses* is one of the stated reasons behind Marx's materialist attack on the Hegelian's speculative, egoistic individualism.
Furthermore, according to Marx and Engels, a more properly
economistic approach to art – that is, one with fewer hesitations
about acknowledging its monetary interests – could actually result
in somewhat *better* works of art than those produced under highly

idealized and fanciful aesthetic regimes. In (the fully bourgeois) Paris, 'the great demand for vaudeville and novels [has] brought about the organisation of work for their production; [and] this organisation at any rate yields something better than its "unique" competitors in Germany'.[37] Is Marx not contradicting himself by saying that there is something artistically *better* in commercially produced novels demanded by the bourgeoisie? Is he not renouncing his earlier view, as expressed in his journalism, that art is debased and degraded through subjection to and instrumentalization by the market? Or is this another instance of his supposedly absolute *epistemological break* with all vestiges of his early Hegelian, humanistic years? None of the above – here Marx and Engels are simply claiming that the products of the commercial publishing and theatrical markets in the more economically and politically developed France are *only* better than those of a German scene still not fully freed from the speculative or Idealistic mental interregnum between an expiring feudalism and an emerging capitalism. Realist French fiction may be generally more tolerable and more artistically advanced, according to Marx, than many (and certainly not all) Romantic German poems – including, perhaps, his own juvenilia – but, ultimately, as seen in his fierce mockery of *The Mysteries of Paris* and his subsequent derision of the French bourgeoisie and their *phantom Paris*, the art of the French bourgeoisie, even if marginally *better* than the *nonsense* being spouted by the Germans, is still very much an abject, degraded ideological instrument.

Before exploring what an undegraded art with an intrinsic value may be – an art that would result from/in the liberation of *artistic talent in the broad mass of people* – I would like to return briefly to the above-quoted passage regarding Raphael, to clarify that Marx's materialist view of art, from 1844–1845 onwards, is not *antihumanistic* and *economico-deterministic*. When Marx and Engels say that Raphael's frescoes *depended on* and were *determined* by the material milieu (of modes of production, divisions of labour, etc.), they do not do so in an absolute or total sense. In their own words, Raphael's work *greatly* but *not* entirely depended on the economic condition of Rome, and it was determined by socioeconomic factors only *as much as any other artist*. Marx and Engels' intention is to rescue the artist from the ultrahumanist abstractions of Idealism and Romanticism, and not to condemn the artist to the dictates of inhuman, mechanistic economic determinism. As such, it is important to take into account that, approximately contemporaneous with cowriting *The German Ideology*, Marx notes that one of the benefits of the socialist agenda for the curtailment of private property – insofar as it would emancipate us from the 'stupid and one-sided' obsession with accruing more capital and individual wealth – is the cultivation of 'the richness of subjective *human* sensibility'.[38] This celebration of *human sensibility*, and Marx's accompanying statements such as 'the most beautiful music has no sense for the unmusical ear',[39] should not be seen as an adherence to Kant's theory of taste and judgement – even though it clearly owes something to Kant's terminology. Marx is quick to point out that, contra Kant, the senses too have their own materiality and history, and that 'the *forming* of the five senses is a labour of the entire history of the world down to the present'.[40] A *musical ear*, and the *beautiful* music that it may discern – and, perhaps à la Kant, the actual music that a musical ear may one day help produce – is not a matter of individual taste, but the outcome of a socially situated and historically materialized aesthetics in the human subject.

For Marx, the emancipated *human subject* is very different to the *unique individual ego* (or identity) found in the Young Hegelian or bourgeois discourses. Marx's *subject* is not the embodiment of an intangible or transcendent human spirit but the manifestation of human interactions with and responses to material, political and historical circumstances. What Marx is proposing, therefore, is not an antihumanism according to which humans possess no ability to sense and make (true, intrinsically valuable) art in the midst of the material conditions of the world, but *a new kind* of humanism that rejects many untenable claims of the philosophical traditions preceding him, such as the account of the human as possessing a consciousness utterly free from the power of ideolo-

gy, or the transcendent version of human sensibility which cele-
brates the (very tasteful and aesthetically refined) individual, ele-
vated above corporeal vulgarity.

In a work of journalism from 1844, and in what may be read as
a challenge to traditional (Kantian and Hegelian) aesthetics, Marx
ruthlessly lampoons a liberal English economist's rhetorical evoca-
tion of a passage by Francis Bacon in which an individual's ability
to temper judgement with wisdom is expressed through the metaphor of mountain climbing, reaching 'the summit of knowledge
where rest and pure air may be enjoyed, where Nature may be
viewed in all her beauty'.[41] Marx's immediate response to this
discourse is both an attack on the economist's palpable avoidance
of the actual and nonmetaphoric outcomes of the capitalist system
that the economist advocates, as well as a direct assault on the
aestheticians' preoccupations with the beautiful and the agreeable:

> The *pure air* of the pestilential atmosphere of English base-
> ment dwellings! The *great natural beauty* of the fantastic rags
> in which the English poor are clothed and of the faded, shriv-
> eled flesh of the women worn out by work and want; the chil-
> dren lying on dung-heaps; the stunted monsters produced by
> overwork in the mechanical monotony of the factories! The
> most charming *final details of practice*: prostitution, murder
> and the gallows![42]

It is important to note that Marx is not denying the domain of
the aesthetic – as noted earlier, he believes in the *richness of
subjective human sensibility* – but that, for him, the aesthetic in
the modern world has very little to do with our perception of the
(figurative and remote) beauty of Nature and suchlike, a beauty
which provides an apologist for capitalism with (literally) lofty
metaphors for advancing his ideology. The aesthetic sensibility of
the modern capitalist world is instead shaped by the *atmosphere*
and colors and shapes of deprivation, injustice and inequality.
Therefore, when it comes to aesthetics, as with art, Marx proposes
a radically materialist theory which undermines the dominant

speculative and ideological perspectives. He neither reduces art to an entirely economical exercise nor does he deny the potential for a human subject to possess and develop a sensibility for making art. But if art's objectifications and ideological abuses are basically things that develop historically and materially with the economic developments of our societies, then is art not destined for annihilation or total ideological objectification in the age of capitalism? Is art not doomed to lose its true, intrinsic value entirely? And, at any rate, what is Marx's own theory regarding such a value? And can it survive or be reinvented in our world? Marx's answers to these key questions require nothing less than a profound new definition of the meaning of art in tandem with a new theory of revolutionary communism.

NOTES

1. Marx and Friedrich Engels, *The Holy Family: Critique of Critical Critique* (Honolulu: University Press of the Pacific, 2002), 85.
2. Ibid.
3. Ibid, 78.
4. Ibid.
5. Ibid, 79.
6. Ibid, 81.
7. Ibid, 84.
8. Ibid, 223.
9. Ibid, 239.
10. Ibid, 240.
11. Ibid, 221.
12. Ibid, 102.
13. Ibid, 220.
14. Ibid, 248.
15. Ibid, 256–57.
16. Ibid, 257.
17. Ibid, 260.
18. I am, of course, referring to the thesis promoted by Louis Althusser, advocated by his followers and opposed by a number of other theo-

rists. For a list of these works please see the conclusion and the section on further reading at the end of the book.

19. Marx and Engels, *The German Ideology, including Theses on Feuerbach and Introduction to the Critique of Political Economy* (New York: Prometheus Books, 1998), 67.

20. Ibid, 285.

21. Ibid, 284.

22. Ibid, 442.

23. Marx, *Economic and Philosophic Manuscripts of 1844*, trans. Martin Milligan (Moscow: Progress Publishers, 1967), 83.

24. Ibid, 110.

25. Marx, *The Civil War in France* (New York: International Publishers, 1940), 69.

26. Marx, *The German Ideology*, 483.

27. Marx, *The Eighteenth Brumaire of Louis Napoleon*, trans, D. D. L. (New York: Mondial, 2005), 27.

28. Ibid: 448.

29. Adam Smith, quoted in Marx, *The Poverty of Philosophy: Answer to the 'Philosophy of Poverty' by M. Proudhon* (Peking: Foreign Languages Press, 1978), 124.

30. Marx and Engels, *The German Ideology*, 414.

31. Ibid, 416.

32. Ibid.

33. Ibid.

34. Ibid, 416–17.

35. Marx, *Capital*, ed. David McLellan (Oxford: Oxford University Press, 2008), 202.

36. Ibid, 417.

37. Ibid.

38. Marx, *Economic and Philosophic Manuscripts of 1844*, 99–101.

39. Ibid, 101.

40. Ibid.

41. Marx, *Early Writings*, trans. Rodney Livingstone and Gregor Benton (London: Penguin, 1992),406.

42. Ibid.

4

ART AND THE JUGGERNAUT OF CAPITAL

THE WHOLE ECONOMIC SHIT?

As noted previously, it has been suggested that Marx's skirmishes with Hegelianism, and the deep engagements with economic theory that characterize his later work, mark a break with humanism. There is, indeed, no denying that his thinking, his writing and his actions were fast moving in less purely intellectual and more directly political directions. This is in part because he was now being seen as a sufficiently significant threat by the European security apparatuses, due to his journalism which attacked Prussian and other European politicians in the same confronting style that his philosophical writing eviscerated his intellectual opponents. The real sources of many a paranoid European police service's anxiety in the mid-1840s, however, had little to do with the inflammatory rhetoric of radical journalists. The slow pace of liberal democratic reforms, as demanded by an ascendant and obdurate bourgeoisie, and the staunch opposition to these reforms by the older ruling classes of the absolute monarchs, conservative clergy and the old nobility were clearly moving the zeitgeist towards another series of major social conflicts. In addition to this, and perhaps more worryingly for the elites, the increasingly impoverished masses of people – who, despite the promises made by reformers and liberal radicals, had seen their lives become more miserable due to both accelerated, technologically advanced industrial modes of labour exploitation and the exploding costs of living due to the bourgeoisie's rampant consumerism – were becoming politicized and organized. Earth-shattering revolutions which would go far beyond the liberals' demand for free speech, the vote and free trade seemed inevitable, and incorrigibly disobedient journalists like Marx – even if, in actual fact, not much of their writing was being published, let alone distributed and read – found themselves in the crosshairs of police services of most European nations.

By the time of his and his young family's expulsion from their beloved Paris in 1845 and their move to the far drabber but less policed Brussels, Marx, now a father, had indeed become a (somewhat) more involved (if not as yet particularly dangerous) political subject, due to his taking an interest in social activism. His involvement in the utopian communist group, the League of the Just, however, could hardly be considered revolutionary – the group was explicitly nonviolent, had no overt political aspirations and, in a clearly religious fashion, preached the virtues of universal humanism, with its motto being 'All Men Are Brothers'. Nevertheless, the league did draw inspiration from the ideas of the notorious Jacobins of the first French revolution, and it seems obvious that Marx – fast becoming convinced that an inevitable confrontation between the most organized and industrially active section of the masses of the ordinary people (*the proletariat*) and the bourgeoisie was the only true response to the contradictions of modern society and politics – recognized the league's potential for serving as a platform for bringing together international activists and intellectuals with a broadly similar belief in the equality and political capacity of all ordinary, working people. Gradually, Marx – and an increasingly more militant and impatient Engels – would come to dominate the league by first establishing the Communist Correspondent Committee as the league's intellectual core in 1846, and then, having the league's name changed to the Communist

League in 1847, with a new slogan, 'Proletarians of the World – Unite'!

In the same year, Marx and Engels were asked by the league to write a manifesto to publicize the group's sociopolitical vision. The result, *The Communist Manifesto*, would be published the following year, the year that revolutions finally erupted in the German states, France, Italian states, the Austrian Empire, Denmark and Poland. *The Communist Manifesto* does include comments on art, such as a succinct reiteration of a theme from Marx's earlier writings apropos the degradation of art due to professionalism, in the form of the observation that, the modern bourgeoisie 'has stripped of its halo' the work of the poet, 'hitherto honoured and looked up to with reverent awe', as it has 'converted' the poet into one of 'its paid wage-labourers'.[1] It should come as no surprise, however, that the central concern of Marx and Engel's most widely read work is the politically restive climate of the period immediately preceding the 1848 revolutions. If thus far Marx's movement from journalism and theorizing (about, among other things, art and literature) to political activism had been a multifaceted and gradual development, the outbreak of the 1848 revolutions accelerated his desire to see both an end to the dynastic power of the despots of his native Prussia and to also deliver a blow against the might of the bourgeoisie in France. But his ill-fated decision to use funds from the inheritance that he had received from his mother to aid Belgian working-class activists, with the aim of fomenting revolution in Brussels – perhaps by paying for guns, while he and his family, which now included three children, had been made to sell their furniture and linen to pay for essentials – resulted in him being separated from the hotbeds of revolutionary activity in Europe. Arrested and then expelled by the Belgian authorities, expelled by the Prussian police after a brief period in Cologne, and barred from returning to France, the Marxes, with very little left of their funds, were forced to seek asylum in the obstinately unrevolutionary, stable and ostensibly far more conservative realm of Victoria's England.

Marx, although still in his early thirties and still enjoying the full support of the longsuffering Jenny and the loyal Engels, was clearly a changed man. Having failed to take part in a revolution in the European continent, having seen the revolutions either peter out or give way to new reactionary forces, and finding himself in conditions of dire financial difficulty that would often border on penury, he would write far less on the topics that had so occupied his mind prior to his exile in London – the questions of art, literature, consciousness and ideology – and devote himself (mostly but certainly not exclusively) to other, seemingly more pressing intellectual concerns, while attempting to influence European political movements from across the English Channel and selling his journalism to the new radical American newspaper, the *New-York Daily Tribune*, whose editor he had met in Cologne prior to his expulsion from his native land. In Cologne, Marx had tried to resuscitate the *Rheinische Zeitung* – as the *Neue Rheinische Zeitung* – to contribute to the revolutionary zeitgeist, but after the Prussian King Wilhelm VI's successful subversion of the constitutional movement and his imposition of a monarchical constitution on the newly elected Prussian National Assembly, the newspaper had been suppressed. It was in this paper that Marx wrote a series of articles that would be edited and published after his death (by Engels) as a small book titled *The Class Struggle in France*. In one of these articles, while lamenting the stifling of free press across the supposedly freshly democratized Europe, Marx provides a more detailed account of the consequences of writers and journalists being instrumentalized and *stripped of their halo* by a particularly devious marriage of monetary and political prerogatives.

In the new France of the Second Republic, the Party of Order (which, for the first time, combined members of the upper bourgeoisie and the conservative monarchists in the interest of defending 'Order, Property and Religion'), having won more than half the seats in the French National Assembly, introduced a legislation that enforced the payment of *caution money*, a good behaviour bond or a guarantee against the publication of what could be deemed as offensive or defamatory, to be paid by publishers. As

Marx notes, 'the provisions concerning caution money killed the so-called revolutionary press'.[2] None of the small radical newspapers – such as those personally funded by people like Marx himself – could either afford to pay the bond or continue to publish anonymous articles. Anonymous journalism had been popular with the more revolutionary publications, to protect their authors from persecution, but this practice was banned by the new law's provision, since it was promulgated 'that every article of a journal must bear the signature of the author'.[3] The combination of the need for the publishers to financially commit to the *good behaviour* of 'the paid writer, with name, address and description'[4] greatly disempowered the press and turned it into an impotent, monetized *literary* instrument. Marx writes:

> As long as the newspaper press was anonymous, it appeared as the organ of a numberless and nameless public opinion; it was the third power in the state. Through the signature of every article, a newspaper became a mere collection of literary contributions from more or less known individuals. Every article sank to the level of an advertisement. Hitherto the newspapers had circulated as the paper money of public opinion; now they were resolved into more or less bad *solo* bills, whose worth and circulation depended on the credit not only of the drawer but also of the endorser.[5]

Here, as with his and Engels's earlier condemnation of *sterile* German socialists who were mere *literary men*, a publication is seen to lose its power when it becomes a mere *collection of literary contributions*. But this comment should not necessarily be seen as a criticism of literature – although the deleterious involvement of so many highly esteemed literary figures such as Hugo, Lamartine and Chateaubriand (whom Marx referred to, in a letter to Engels, as 'this foolish fop'[6]) in French politics had disappointed and angered many a genuine revolutionary such as Marx – nor should this be seen as a naïve celebration of the efficacy of journalism and the righteousness of *public opinion*. The key insight here concerns the renunciation of a system that reduces writing to the level of *advertisement*. When a writer can be published solely because of the wealth and clout of the publisher who can bear the cost of paying the caution money, and when, at the same time, he or she is transformed (or, perhaps, deformed) from an *organ* of the people into a *literary individual*, then he or she is quite literally devalued. According to Marx's fascinating analogy, such a writer no longer represents public opinion as *representative* paper money represents a claim on a commodity such as gold – that is, as representative of *intrinsic* fiscal value – but becomes something like fiat money, bills whose nonintrinsic, imaginary worth depends entirely on their endorsement by a political power (and an instrument of the financial bourgeoisie) such as a central bank. Such a writer, in other words, possesses no real, *in-itself* value, but only the kind of assumed value that is served by modern banknotes as things with no intrinsic value (i.e., the paper of the notes itself is worthless) purely an instrument of exchange and commercial activity.

During the 1850s, Marx came to believe that the defeats of the revolutionary upheavals of the 1840s – seen most emblematically in the ascendancy of the opportunistic and authoritarian Louis-Napoléon Bonaparte, first as the president of the new French republic and then as the country's self-proclaimed emperor à la his uncle, the first Napoléon – resulted from economic factors. And central to the power, demands and resilience of capitalism and the capitalist bourgeoisie were the features, origins and qualities of the bourgeoisie's financial wealth or capital itself – capital as investment, as power over the means of production, and as that which is procured from the exploitation of the working class, or what Marx came to describe as the extraction of *surplus-value*. Far from finding an immediate answer to the riddle of capital's resources and consequences, however, Marx found himself overwhelmed – and also obsessed – by the immensity of his task, by the huge volume of economic theories and industrial records and data kept at London's research libraries, as well as the grandeur of his project's ambition, the desire to produce the definitive account of the modern world's material reality, and, by so doing, equip the proletariat with a *science* – not simply another dubious ideology – for understanding and countering the bourgeoisie's catastrophic, magical weapon: capital.

Mature Marx's intense concentration on his economics project – which has been referred to as simply his 'economics' or, in his own words, the *'whole economic shit'* – may have made the once-gregarious, outgoing journalist into a more introverted, solitary figure. His terribly bitter personal and political feuds with the other German exiles – which at one point resulted in a physical duel – were in part responsible for the disintegration and disbandment of the Communist League in 1852. Meanwhile, Marx's personal life was beset by unprecedented material hardship, illness and tragedy, including the death of his eight-year-old son Edgar from consumption.

By the end of the first decade of his life in London, the world-weary forty-year-old Marx had come to find something of a refuge from both the miseries of daily life and the failures of his political ambitions by immersing himself in research and working in the British Museum Reading Room. In between having to write and sell articles on European politics to the *New-York Daily Tribune* – which entailed his having to learn and write in English – and dreading the fact that he, who had once scoffed at the prospect of having to earn a living from writing, was now a thoroughly *proletarianized wage slave*, Marx maintained the energy and the drive to continue with the rigorous study of the economic roots of the modern capitalist system and the question of capital, and with drafting his revolutionary magnum opus.

ART AND CAPITALIST DEVELOPMENT

Although Marx's constantly expanding economics project meant that he would no longer extensively focus on the arts, he would not go on to theorize solely on economic questions such as surplus-value extraction and, by so doing, reduce human subjects to mere objects or data for economic analysis – as many a modern economist would be inclined to do – nor would he forgo his interest in the humanities. Indeed, one of his most succinct and important reflections on the arts can be found in the unfinished manuscript *Grundrisse*, written in 1857–1858, the draft *outline* of his 'economics'.

Here, Marx reiterates a point made more than a decade earlier about the difference between the products of artistic production and those of nonartistic production, but he now firmly places the arts in the context of his increasingly elaborate theory of historical materialism which, if not Hegelian in spirit, is very much a materialist extrapolation occasioned by a Hegelian logic. Initially, Marx sets out to 'clarify' and make 'less puzzling' the paradoxical phenomenon of highly developed forms of artistic production such as Homeric epics or Shakespearian drama as found in comparatively 'undeveloped' pre- or early-modern societies of ancient Greece and Renaissance England.[7] He writes:

> In the case of the arts, it is well known that certain periods of their flowering are out of all proportion to the general development of society, hence also to the material foundation, the skeletal structure as it were, of its organization. For example, the Greeks compared to the moderns or also Shakespeare. It is even recognized that certain forms of art, e.g. the epic, can no longer be produced in their world epoch-making, classical stature as soon as the production of art, as such, begins; that is, that certain significant forms within the realm of the arts are possible only at an underdeveloped stage of artistic development. If this is the case with the relation between different kinds of art within the realm of the arts, it is already less puzzling that it is the case in the relation of the entire realm to the general development of society. The difficulty consists only in the general formulation of these contradictions. As soon as they have been specified, they are already clarified.[8]

By dialectically splitting the unitary phenomenon of art into two opposing components – the *forms* of art versus the *realm* of art – Marx is applying to the question of art (what Engels saw as)

Hegel's first law of dialectics. In what may recall Kant's belief in art's value in expanding *mental powers*, Marx seems to be suggesting that, with the expansion of the realm of art thanks to the genius of an *epoch-making* initiatory form such as the epic poem – and, of course, also due to society's gradual economic developments – the second law of dialectics is activated: the quantitative change in the realm of art (e.g., the larger medieval or modern literary epochs that are in some ways *made* by or *begin* with the ancient epic) result in a qualitative change in the forms of art, and the *flowering* of a form such as the epic, despite its *classical stature*, starts to wane. Finally, and à la the third materialist law of dialectics, the epic, having participated in bringing about the epoch or realm of a more developed literature (e.g., the novel) and having, as such, become its own negation (by inspiring the development of the rival form of the novel), comes to an end and can *no longer be produced*. Put most simply, the epic becomes a victim to its own artistic success.

And it is not only because of the dialectic of the epic poem, but also due to what Marx noted in the above-quoted passage as *the relation of the entire realm [of art] to the general development of society* that, even if modern or recent cultures and societies are in many ways more advanced than ancient ones, their authors – even their *best* authors – cannot compose masterful epics in the manner of Homer and Virgil. In another version of his 'economics' from 1861 to 1863, *Theories of Surplus-Value*, and while commenting on a critic of Adam Smith, Marx accuses that critic of not having a proper understanding of how society and ideology develop according to a given mode of production. The critic does not see that one of the capitalist bourgeoisie's 'ideological component parts' is 'free spiritual production'.[9] I will elaborate on the specific and very crucial place of *spirituality* as such in Marx's philosophy of art a little later, and for now note that the term *free spiritual production* here does not have religious qualities and is an English translation of the German phrase which has been translated also as 'free intellectual production'.[10] The intellectual or spiritual or, at any rate, *mental or nonphysical* production under capitalism is *free* in tandem with industrial capitalist modes of production's demand for *free labourers* – who must *voluntarily* sell their labour-power to employers and, hence, enable the bourgeoisie to extract surplus-value from their labour without the bourgeois boss having to provide for all of the labourer's needs as would have been the case under slavery or serfdom – which then results in a decline in less *free*, more formally disciplined or rigid artforms such as traditional or metric verse. Marx writes:

> [C]apitalist production is hostile to certain branches of spiritual [or mental] production, for example, art and poetry. If this is left out of account, it opens the way to the illusion of the French in the eighteenth century which has been so beautifully satirised by Lessing. Because we are further ahead than the ancients in mechanics, etc., why shouldn't we be able to make an epic too? And the *Henriade* in place of the *Iliad*![11]

It would not be difficult to mock, with Lessing and Marx, the great Voltaire's misguided attempt to write an epic poem, modelled on the *Iliad*, about the life of a venerated French king. The *Henriade* is, by all accounts, a run-of-the-mill, forgettable work. The question of capitalism's hostility to art in general, however, is something that has been stated quite simplistically in this passage. Are the modern bourgeois novels and glamourous stage spectacles of Marx's own time – and immensely commercial cinema, popular music and digital entertainments of our own, not to mention the very lucrative *high art* scenes of classical music and visual arts dealership – far from being the objects of capitalism's antagonism, not in fact the very paragons of money making, surplus-value generating capitalist modes of production? As Marx himself observes, also in *Theories of Surplus-Value*, an artist such as a singer or a writer can indeed be integrated into the capitalist economy and be seen as a *productive* worker according to a capitalist definition of production. He writes:

> [T]he literary proletarian of Leipzig who fabricates books (for example, *Compendia of Economics*) under the direction of this

publisher is a productive worker, for his production is subordinated to capital in advance and takes place only because it increases that capital. A singer who sells her song on her own is an unproductive worker. But the same singer, commissioned by an *entrepreneur* to sing in order to make money for him, is a productive worker. For she produces capital.[12]

Industrial capitalism's *hostility to art and poetry* should therefore be qualified as a hostility towards *certain branches* or certain (commercially) unprofitable forms of art such as the epic poem – and, indeed, perhaps poetry *tout court* – and not towards all forms or the entire realm of art. And occasionally, as we have seen in *The Communist Manifesto*, even the poet may be *stripped of his or her halo* and become a *literary proletarian*. As noted in the most famous published form of his 'economics', *Capital, Volume One*, even an artist as obscenely successful and hysterically revered (during Marx's life) as Richard Wagner is, ultimately, a wage labourer who must instrumentalize his art or sell his labour-power to the (cultural) capitalists because he does not own his own means of production. Without referring to the specifics of Wagner's desperate attempts at selling his capacity as a composer and a conductor to wealthy patrons and buyers (to, for example, garner financial support from the King of Bavaria for building the Bayreuth Festival Theatre), Marx notes that 'not even "the musician of the future"' – a sarcastic reference to the title of one of Wagner's essays – 'can live upon future products',[13] that is, even the deified Wagner is not able to attract funding or capital for his future operas without first selling his ability to produce operas or, in effect, without first becoming an employee of the King of Bavaria. The artist, as free as he or she may be in seeking patrons and buyers for his or her art, is not free from the need to have to sell his or her labour-power to make art, and therefore comes to *belong to* and be restrained by this material condition. As also noted in *Capital, Volume One*, 'the actor during the whole course of the play belongs to the stage'.[14]

In one of the most powerful passages towards the end of *Capital, Volume One*, Marx suggests that the process of labour exploitation or surplus-value extraction is inherently antagonistic towards the aesthetic *charm* and the *intellectual* modalities that are most readily associated with the artistic. This antagonism is concomitant with the apocalyptic horrors of modern capitalism, with the conditions that make it *historically inevitable* for the working people to (eventually) unite and revolt against the despotism of capital. Marx writes:

> [W]ithin the capitalist system all methods for raising the social productiveness of labour are brought about at the cost of the individual labourer; all means for the development of production transform themselves into means of domination over, and exploitation of, the producers; they mutilate the labourer into a fragment of a man, degrade him to the level of an appendage of a machine, destroy every remnant of charm in his work and turn it into a hated toil; they estrange from him the intellectual potentialities of the labour-process in the same proportion as science is incorporated in it as an independent power; they distort the conditions under which he works, subject him during the labour-process to a despotism the more hateful for its meanness; they transform his life-time into working-time, and drag his wife and child beneath the wheels of the Juggernaut of capital. [15]

It would be tempting to read this passage as a wholesale refutation of the possibility to produce anything like art, anything with *charm* or an *intellectual potential*, under capitalism. How could one possibly care about art while struggling to survive under *the wheels of the Juggernaut of capital*? It is important to note, however, that here – and, as we shall see, throughout his oeuvre – Marx emphasizes exploitation and capital's utterly *mean* and *hateful* domination in concert with establishing or strongly implying the existence of the dignity and worth of the labourer's human subjectivity or the labourer's *lifetime*. If the human producer did not possess something like a living wholeness or at least a subjective coherence – or the capacity for such a thing – then how could this person then become *a fragment of a man* as a result of capitalist labour-process? The labourer must possess – in actuality or in potentiality – something *unfragmented or unmutilated* in the first place (which one may call, however cautiously, *humanity*) if the process of exploitation is to be lamented for its *mutilation of the labourer into a fragment of a man*. I would not be able to note or complain about being fragmented, in other words, if I were fragmented to begin with, or if fragmentation were an a priori of my consciousness. This is clearly not the case in even the late Marx. In this passage, he clearly indicates that there is an *intellectual potential* in labour, if we are to hold true the statement that the capitalist means of surplus-value generation *estrange from the worker the intellectual potential of his or her work*. As such, the intellectual potential of production and finding charm in one's work – qualities which, as I've suggested, are consonant with artistic production – possess their own concrete actuality, and despite all the degradations and miseries of capitalism, are not entirely erased or annihilated. If these were annihilated, and if this annihilation had become a natural given of our condition, then neither we nor Marx would find anything objectionable or hateful about this annihilation. We would, in fact, be indifferent towards being crushed under the wheels of the Juggernaut of capital because we would not know or want any better. And such an acquiescence is neither the case in Marx's writings or in the modern world of social unrest and revolutions.

Therefore, despite Marx's low opinion of Wagner's music or his mockery of Voltaire's epic poetry, it would be inaccurate to say that for him art is wholly destined to intrinsic mediocrity or qualitative degradation under capitalism, irrespective of the degree and kind of *hostility* to which the capitalist modes of production may subject *certain branches of mental production* according to *Theories of Surplus-Value*. Indeed, Marx holds quite a number of modern works of art in very high esteem. In an article written for the *New-York Daily Tribune* in 1854 while working on his 'economics', Marx openly praises explicitly bourgeois Victorian novels' ability to produce *truths* that he formulates in his own powerful phrasing as an epigram *fixed* to the entire bourgeois class:

> The present splendid brotherhood of fiction-writers in England, whose graphic and eloquent pages have issued to the world more political and social truths than have been uttered by all the professional politicians, publicists and moralists put together, have described every section of the middle class from the 'highly genteel' annuitant and Fundholder who looks upon all sorts of business as vulgar, to the little shopkeeper and lawyer's clerk. And how have Dickens and Thackeray, Miss Brontë and Mrs. Gaskell painted them? As full of presumption, affectation, petty tyranny and ignorance; and the civilized world has confirmed their verdict with the damning epigram that it has fixed to this class that 'they are servile to those above, and tyrannical to those beneath them.'[16]

As sincere as Marx's appreciation for these Victorian novelists seems, it should be noted that, in the context of a discussion of artistic value, the *truths* or values offered by these novels could be potentially more instrumental than intrinsic. These truths and what they reveal about the commercial as well as the petty bourgeois may be said to be the revelations or representations of existing *political* and *social* realties, and not the productions of (new) ideas and truths, or at least not in the Platonic sense of *truth*. Based on Marx's appraisal of the novels' acknowledgement of the reality (of the minds and characters of a range of bourgeois types) it may be said that this fiction is a literary-aesthetic instrument for gaining a knowledge of social reality, and not a condition for the production of the novels' *own*, intrinsic reality. So it may be said that here Marx praises and values these *splendid* works not as novels per se but as unofficial interventions in a sociological discourse, called forth by the shortcomings of the official sociological analyses by politicians and others. Had the official – perhaps scientific as opposed to either *moralist* or literary – analysts of Victorian society been able to offer suitably *graphic and eloquent* accounts of industrialized England's social classes, would there still have been a need for novels such as those by Elizabeth Gaskell or Charles Dickens or the occasion for Marx to praise them? This passage, at any rate, refutes the implication, as found in the *Grundrisse* and *Theories of Surplus-Value*, that for Marx all art produced either in modern Europe or under capitalism is bereft of any value whatsoever. In an 1869 letter to Engels, and accompanying his second copy of Denis Diderot's satirical novel *Rameau's Nephew* as a gift for his friend, Marx describes the novel as a 'unique masterpiece'.[17] Even poetry – Romantic poetry from the speculative and idealist milieu of Germany which one would assume Marx, who had long stopped writing poetry, had completely left behind – is not entirely incapable of *flowering* in the age of surplus-value accumulation and can be used to show complex *political and social truths*. In another article written during the same period for the same newspaper, Marx quotes a poem from Goethe's *West-östlicher Divan* to illustrate the dialectic of the British colonization of India, to show that the '*Quals*' (Eng. 'torment') brought about by the '*Herrschaft*' ('dominion') of the brutal conquering power (either the Asiatic conqueror Timur or Tamerlane in Goethe's poem, or the British Empire during Marx's life) would result in its own negation; by destroying traditional, feudal powers in India, the empire creates the conditions for 'a fundamental revolution in the social state of Asia' and, therefore, as the poem would have it, the '*lust*' ('joy') of eventual emancipation from both Asian feudalism and European colonialism.[18]

Such a negation of a negation is, as mentioned before, at play in Marx's description of the epic poem in the brief albeit dense and pivotal discussion of art in the *Grundrisse*. And while ancient poetry such as Homer's may no longer be producible under capitalism, the continuing appeal and power of such poetry poses another, even more challenging question. Marx states that 'the difficulty lies not in understanding that the Greek arts and epic are bound up with certain forms of social development' but that 'they still afford us artistic pleasure and that in a certain aspect they count as a norm and as an unattainable model'.[19] As Marx notes, the age of ancient warfare – the content of much epic poetry – of

Grecian hoplites and chariots came to an end with 'powder and lead,' and the primacy of the oral from of the epic – 'the song and the saga' – too was terminated 'with the printer's bar'.[20] And yet the likes of the *Iliad* and the *Odyssey* have retained their value as both *pleasurable* and as supreme artistic *models*.[21] Recalling Aristotle and Kant, we can say that both these values are instrumental – art-as-catharsis serves a psychological, nonartistic imperative, and art-as-model is a means to the techne-mechanical end of making more (developed) works of art – but, since neither ancient warfare nor ancient mediatic technologies hold any (instrumental) value for us now, why is it that the ancient poems remain so valuable – pleasurable and seminal – in the modern age?

This question and Marx's formulation of it in the *Grundrisse* are, in my opinion, one of the most important – and, in its own way, *epic* – questions posed in the Western philosophy of art. It shows the exceptional development and sophistication of Marx's thinking about art, perhaps occasioned by the years of struggling with the *whole economic shit*. And yet, his immediate answer to this question in the *Grundrisse* is nothing if not disappointing. Here Marx claims that, despite our modern capitalist socioeconomic, technological and ideological conditions being vastly different to those of the early poets, we still find their works *pleasurable* and worthy of imitation because these works come from 'the historic childhood of humanity'; and, in the same way that an adult may 'find joy in the child's naïveté', a subject of the more historically and materially advanced society may find oneself under 'the eternal charm' of the artistic products of 'the unripe social conditions' of ancient Greece.[22]

I find such a sentimental argument difficult to accept, particularly as it comes from a thinker as rigorous and thorough as Marx. *Charming* as a child may be, does an encounter with him or her provide real pleasure, which, as Aristotle would have it, would only come from an encounter with *pity and fear*, not with *naïveté*? And, as much as one may admire and encourage a child (and his or her *unripe* works), does one come to *model* one's own work on that of the child, no matter how delightful or, again, how charming one may find that child's creativity?

NOTES

1. Marx and Engels, *The Communist Manifesto* (Hammondsworth: Penguin Books, 1986), 82.

2. Marx, *The Class Struggle in France* (New York: International Publishers, 1964), 138.

3. Ibid.

4. Ibid, 139.

5. Ibid, 138.

6. Marx, quoted in Marx and Engels, *Marx & Engels on Literature and Art*, eds. Lee Baxandall and Stefan Morawski (St Louis; Milwaukee: Telos Press, 1973), 140.

7. Marx, *Grundrisse: Foundations of the Critique of Political Economy*, trans. Martin Nicolaus (London: Penguin Books, 1993), 110.

8. Ibid.

9. Marx, *Theories of Surplus-Value*, *Marxist Internet Archive*, accessed 14 January 2018;https://www.marxists.org/archive/marx/works/1863/theories-surplus-value.

10. Marx, quoted in *Marx & Engels on Literature and Art*, 64.

11. Marx, *Theories of Surplus-Value*.

12. Marx, *Theories of Surplus Value*, trans. G. A. Bonner and Emile Burns (London: Lawrence & Wishart, 1951), 186.

13. Marx, *Capital*, ed. David McLellan (Oxford: Oxford University Press, 2008), 109.

14. Ibid, 176.

15. Ibid, 362.

16. Marx, *Dispatches for the New York Tribune: Selected Journalism of Karl Marx*, ed. James Ledbetter (London: Penguin Books, 2007), 143.

17. Marx, 'Letter from Marx to Engels in Manchester', *Marxist Internet Archive*, accessed 21 January 2018,https://www.marxists.org/archive/marx/works/1869/letters/69_04_15-abs.htm.

18. Marx, *Dispatches for the New York Tribune*, 218–19.

19. Marx, *Grundrisse*, 111.

20. Ibid.

21. Ibid.
22. Ibid.

5

WHY WE MAKE ART

WAS MARX WRONG?

I shall not dwell on my disagreement with Marx when it comes to an appreciation of a *child's naïveté*. I readily agree with him that the pleasure that may be gained from reading, viewing, hearing or, in short, *consuming* art is indeed one genuine (albeit instrumental) reason why we value art. Furthermore, I will now admit that, while the previous chapter's summary of Marx's theory of art as put forward in the *Grundrisse* is not inaccurate – and it clearly conforms to some of the commonly held views of Marx's supposedly *stageist* and progressive theory of historical materialism – it is also an (intentionally) *incomplete* summary. What I have left out of my précis is Marx's crucial discussion of *artistic production*, nestled between his proposal of the artforms' paradoxical relationship with the development of the realm of art and his ostensibly Romanic designation of the possibly clichéd image of infantile innocence as the source of art's aesthetic pleasures.

I have done this so that I may focus solely on the pivotal question of production in Marx's philosophy of art with more deliberation, and to also convey the problems of an image of Marx – and, indeed, of Marxism – which is not conversant with the key tenet of his philosophy from his earliest years to his very last writings: the question of human production. It should come as no surprise that, in the *Grundrisse*, Marx, the most important theorist of working-class political power in the nineteenth century, and one of the key historical champions of the indispensable force and integrity of work and production in the world, emphasizes the arts' essential value as that which is *produced by real people* prior to addressing the pleasurable or *charming* effects on hypothetical consumers of the artist's products. And yet, it is very much an image of Marx as primarily a theorist of market economy, bourgeois social relations and commercialization, that is, Marx as a theorist of how products are circulated and not how – or, very importantly, why – they are produced in the first place, which has dominated the interpretations of his philosophy, particularly in the works of those who accuse Marx of making mistaken or unconvincing arguments, an example of which was given in my own analysis at the end of the previous chapter.

One of the key *mistakes* that many (even self-described Marxist) commentators have found in mature Marx's philosophy concerns the labour theory of value. (Which, incidentally, is not entirely Marx's own and was adapted by him from the work of, among others, the liberal economist David Ricardo.) The labour theory of value posits labour-time or the time that it takes to make something as the basis of the exchange-value of a product; however, if value is simply that which is demanded and determined by a consumer or by the market – price – then it can indeed be shown that this theory is wrong. The prices of things in our world are clearly not the expression of the time or labour spent in producing them, and this is particularly evident in the arts. As we all know, a hasty, clumsy doodle by a famous artist has a much greater price than an entire life's worth of sumptuous oil paintings by an unknown artist. But this irregularity or 'the whole mystery of commodities'[1] is *precisely* what Marx diagnoses, criticizes and confronts in his critique of capitalist political economy and in the best-known version of his 'economics', *Capital, Volume One*, which was finally completed and published in 1867.

If one were to state this immense book's key argument as simplistically as possible, one would perhaps say that, according to Marx, the cost of labour or of labour-power is made variable and relative in the modern world – for example, workers are made to work longer workdays, or they are made to work more intensively – so that the bourgeois can extract surplus-value from the labour-process and turn (less) money into (more) capital. Marx seeks (and, I believe, succeeds brilliantly) to show that under capitalism labour-time becomes a malleable thing, and it is precisely due to this that after articulating Ricardo's classical formulation – that, *in the first instance*, labour-time is the only property common to different products which makes them at all exchangeable (or, in one sense of the word, *valuable*) – Marx then shows us that in a world driven by the complex interests of capital, value becomes subject to capitalism's central project of turning labour-time into a variability and that value can therefore no longer be measured in labour-time. Marx never suggests that the value of work or of the product of work is factually expressed in the universal equivalent form of money or in price; and he never ceases to remind his readers that real people's labour-power and labour-time become abstract (and, ultimately, hidden, *distorted* and *mutilated*) for the purposes of commodification, exploitation and surplus-value extraction, in accordance with the interests of the investors, bosses, consumers and so on against the interests of the ordinary workers and producers themselves. While according to the classical economists – whose theories provide Marx with an entry into the murky milieu of economics – the quantity of labour should *in theory* determine or at least ground the exchange-value of a commodity, in the practices of our capitalist world, exchange-value is instead manipulated and reconstituted by the exploitative quality of the process that has no aim other than boosting profit or capital.

It surprises me that erudite commentators have accused Marx of assuming that the price of a product is determined by the time spent on making it, when, as I think it can be seen from an even cursory reading of *Capital, Volume One*, Marx makes an avowedly contradictory analysis – that, under capitalism, such a direct, proportional relationship between labour and value is the *very thing* that has ceased to exist. I don't know how to entirely account for such a basic, baffling misreading of *Capital, Volume One* by Marx's critics, but I believe such misinterpretations are greatly assisted by what I've depicted throughout this book as a faulty belief in the mature Marx's supposedly fundamental break with all aspects of humanism found in his younger philosophy. If Marx had already undergone such a total break prior to *Capital, Volume One*, then in his view exploitation could not have the capacity for abstracting and distorting an a priori human laboured activity, because such an activity (or any kind of labour other than the minimal requirement to start off an automated process of surplus-value generation) would simply not exist. And if this were the case, exploitation would no longer be *exploitation*, but a benign engine for turning money into more money. Such a view of capitalism would be frankly absurd, or at least a version of some of the most far-fetched fantasies of today's neoliberal champions of *casino capitalism*. This view, at any rate, is absolutely not shared by Marx, and nothing of the sort is found in even Marx's most *economic-deterministic* texts. What we find in his writings, instead, is the consistent application and development of certain themes across his entire body of work, themes with perhaps overly humanistic origins (grounded in the speculative ontologies of German Idealism) which Marx, while subjecting them to his own brand of materialism, never entirely detaches from their specifically human character. And among these is the crucial concept of *alienation* or estrangement, a major point of continuity between the younger and older thinker's writings.

ART AGAINST ALIENATION

Alienation is a topic that features heavily in Marx's writing both before and after the supposed *epistemological break*, and it is this theme which provides us with a central concept for understanding Marx's theory of artistic value and the striking possibility for art's value to be *both intrinsic and useful*. I believe that for Marx, art's instrumental values – be they the ancient epic poet's surprising ability to still afford us charm and pleasure, or the modern English novelists' conviction to convey social and political realities, or a German poet's gift for conveying complex dialectical themes in a handful of terse poetic lines – depend on literature's and art's deeper, noninstrumental value, which is connected to what we have already encountered as the other of the processes of capitalist accumulation that *estrange from the worker the intellectual potentialities of the labour-process*. Art's important instrumental values are occasioned by its intrinsic value as denoted by the *un*estranged and *un*estranging intellectual potential of *concrete artistic labour*.

Both terms *alienation* and *estrangement* have been used for translating the German words *entäussern* and *entfremden* as found in Marx's writings, notably in the essay titled, posthumously, '*Die Enfermdete Arbeit*' (Engl. 'Estranged/alienated Labour), written during the younger Marx's formative years in Paris, in 1844. Here, in tandem with his gravitation towards communism, working-class radicalism, Anglo-Scottish economic theory and his growing awareness of the foundational albeit suppressed capacity of the worker in the modern world, Marx proposes that the bourgeois employers, investors and financiers make money and extract profit from workers and employees not through forced labour or the collection of feudal seigniorial dues, but via the less detectable but far more effective and modern method of commodification. (Marx, as we have seen, will later explain how precisely commodification degrades workers and enriches the bourgeois through the introduction of the motif of surplus-value in the 1850s.) When what the worker has produced (an object, a service, etc.) is removed from the worker's immediate sphere of production and is entered into the market of consumer demands as something with a price, its value becomes subject to the law of supply and demand – the higher the supply, the lower the demand – as a result of which 'the worker becomes all the poorer the more wealth he produces, the more his production increases in power and range'.[2]

And, hence, 'the object which labour produces – labour's product – confronts it as something *alien*, as a *power independent* of
the producer'.[3]

While earlier German Idealists had associated alienation with
the basic premise of social existence – and with concomitant exis-
tential phenomena, such as dogmatic religious faith – Marx locates
it in the specific milieu of the capitalist mode of production. He
founds a critique of estrangement not in the 'philanthropy of atheism' but in taking note of the immediate materiality of things in
the modern world, in 'the movement of *private property*' which,
in another piece of writing from 1844, he describes as 'the material sensuous expression of *estranged human* life'.[4] Marx notes that
(in the modern, capitalist world) art is among the '*particular*
modes of production' that come under the 'general law' of private
property and this law's *movement* which consists of 'consumption
and production'.[5] And in order to explicate how precisely the capitalist appropriation of labour functions and results in deep and
debilitating alienation – in which 'man (the worker) no longer feels
himself to be freely active'[6] – Marx introduces a crucial definition
of *concrete* or *nonalienated* human labour.

Concrete labour or production is not primarily a professional or
commercial activity, but what we as a species do owing to our
basic dependence on both organic nature (animals, plants, etc.)
and inorganic nature (earth, water, air, etc.) for survival. As such,
production, in the first instance, is what we do to make the objects
of nature *useful* for meeting our most immediate and pressing
needs. Furthermore, we participate in this concrete and nonalienated production consciously and freely (when and where not subjected to capitalist or other alienating modes of production) because, while engaged in satisfying our basic needs like animals, we
are, unlike animals, aware of our actions and our needs, due to our
universality or our cognitive ability to recognize ourselves as
members of our collective or universal species.

This account of *conscious* and *free* production should not be
dismissed as Romantic or Idealist, liberal or naïvely Aristotelian.
Marx's account certainly owes something to Aristotle – or to a

general theory of (nonslave) production as a voluntary act in the pursuit of satisfying needs – but for him production is subject to (historically) specific modes of production (feudalism, capitalism, etc., including, indeed, various kinds of slave labour exploitation) with their concomitant divisions of labour and social relations which alter, if not the basic impulse, then the forms, the content and the quality of production contra Aristotle or a simple version of a *timeless* humanism. The (Aristotelian theory of the) satisfaction of needs is a tenet of Marx's own theory of production, but, due to the other, equally important materialist and dialectical tenets of his thought, he sees the quantitative and hence qualitative changes made to the ancient kernel of production as fundamental. For Marx, while we produce things with the general aim of potentially satisfying our needs, our actual needs and how we produce things change dramatically from one historical epoch to another. And it is in the course of making this perhaps complex definition of production that Marx provides a highly pertinent and startling observation about the work of art:

> The life of the species, both in man and in animals, consists physically in the fact that man (like the animal) lives on inorganic nature; and the more universal man is compared with the animal, the more universal is the sphere of inorganic nature on which he lives. Just as plants, animals, stones, the air, light, etc., constitute a part of human consciousness in the realm of theory, partly as objects of natural science, partly as objects of art – his spiritual inorganic nature, spiritual nourishment which he must first prepare to make it palatable and digestible – so too in the realm of practice they constitute a part of human life and human activity.[7]

A quick reading of this passage would suggest that Marx is merely advancing a somewhat more scientific version of Hegel's belief in the spiritual value of art. But a closer analysis suggests something else entirely. Spirituality may be defined (at least from a materialist perspective) as a naïve albeit necessary primitive belief in the spiritual power or life of inanimate, nonliving or inor-

ganic objects or abstract concepts (e.g., a belief in the existence of
a god of the sea, or a goddess of wisdom, and so on) and, as such,
spirituality is something that arises, historically, at the same time
that we develop specifically human productive capacities as hunter
gatherers, pastoralists and, finally, village-building agriculturalists
and city-building traders. While, at this point, spirituality seeks to
offer nothing more (or less) than mental *nourishment* contra the
fears and dangers of the nonhuman, natural world that threatens
the survival of early humans, it does not in fact make the natural
world more agreeable or less threatening. If anything, the deifica-
tion of inorganic natural phenomena grants them more (mental)
power over us, a genuinely supernatural and alien power – it is the
primitive manifestation of alienation and ideology – one which we
may then hope to appease through rituals such as worship, offering sacrifices and so on.

According to Marx, spirituality as such is already a part of the
inorganic world that surrounds us, on par with other objects of
inorganic nature (e.g., stones) which we, through practical productive activity (such as stone-cutting), turn into things that are useful
to us (say, stone bricks) as we advance human civilization. And as
stones cannot be used for building houses until they have been cut
into bricks, spirituality too is not (in its initial, highly superstitious
from) *palatable* and *digestible* with regards to our developing
needs – and art is the task or the process of the preparation and
transformation of spirituality into things that we can use in *the
realm of theory*, or as things that we use to help us (begin to)
understand and not simply believe in our environs. We may seek
spiritual nourishment in the same way that nonuniversal organic
beings (animals, plants, etc.) would seek nourishment from inorganic nature (drink water, breathe air, etc.) but, as universal beings conscious of our essence, we need – in addition to water, air,
and so forth – to subject the inorganic objects of our nonmaterial
or spiritual encounters with nature to a process of *theoretical* production in concert with our practical activities. We satisfy this
need for understanding, theorization, ideation and, finally, assimilation or *integration* with the world – and, indeed, with nature –

through practicing art (and, interestingly, also science, although in a way that is intrinsically different to art) to reverse or unravel the alienating mental powers of spirituality. The *nonalienated* and *noninstrumental* value of art, therefore, is found in art being the production of theoretical or intellectual usefulness or use-values out of the spiritual interface between our human consciousness and the immediate nonhumanity of nature.

I do not at all wish to simplify this frankly extraordinary theory of art any more than may be necessary for the purposes of clarification. But I would like to attempt to put this view of art in as succinct a formulation as possible: art produces real, concrete human uses out of our spiritual, mythological and ideological environments – or, out of the beliefs and forms of consciousness that we have inherited from our ancestors – in the form of producing new theories and ideas (or *truths*) as concrete works of art which enable us to comprehend, engage with and live truthfully with and in the world. If spirituality, mythology, religion and modern capitalist ideology all produce different kinds and degrees of alienation, then art is that which is produced for the inherent and fundamental purpose or use-value of unalienating the world, making the world *un*supernatural and assimilating and integrating us with its nature which is, finally, (our own) nature as such.

It is important to emphasize that this capacity is not an instrumentalization of art – an agenda that turns art into a means for an end, removed from the original milieu of artistic production – but it is the very intrinsic *raison d'être* of art, the primary *concrete* reason we make art. Through *abstract labour* we turn our labour-power into a commodity and we therefore turn our labour into an instrument for creating exchange-value (a wage for us, capital for our bosses), that is, into a means to an economic end. Through the *concrete labour* of producing use-value for our primal need to counter the alienating power of (our misunderstandings of) the world around us, we make an art that is neither an economic or ideological instrument, but a direct satisfaction of an immediate mental need. Certain kinds of modern artistic production can, as we have seen, be commodified and turned into profitable production. As noted in *Theories of Surplus-Value*, for example, a 'writer who turns out factory-made stuff for his publisher is a productive worker' in the capitalist, alienated sense of productivity.[8] However, there is another kind of production, which can be seen in the work of an artist whose work is not made to generate surplus-value for a publisher. Here Marx uses the example of a famously seminal, famously commercially undervalued work of literature: 'Milton produced *Paradise Lost* for the same reason a silk worm produces silk. It was an activity of his nature'.[9] Art's value resides, first and foremost, in the site of its human-natural production (and not consumption) and is intrinsic to the productive activity itself, to the struggle against the inorganic, inhuman forces of ideology and alienation.

It may perhaps be difficult to think of spirituality and religion as *inorganic* or *environmental* matter on par with what exists naturally without our intervention, such as water or earth. Is religion (particularly for a staunch materialist like Marx) not a man-made thing? Yes, but that is not how we *perceive* it; seen as ideology, spirituality has the very function of producing a (*false*) consciousness that obfuscates or *inverts* its material genesis. And art (among other kinds of mental production or *truth-procedures*, as Badiou might put it, such as science, each *in their own entirely singular way*) responds to our need to produce ideas and understanding contra the ignorance and alienation caused by ideology. In one of the best-known passages of *The German Ideology*, Marx and Engels write:

> The production of ideas, of conceptions, of consciousness, is at first directly interwoven with the material activity and the material intercourse of men – the language of real life. Conceiving, thinking, the mental intercourse of men at this stage will appear as the direct efflux of their material behavior. The same applies to mental production. . . . Men are the producers of their conceptions, ideas, etc., that is, real, active men, as they are conditioned by a definite development of their productive

forces and of the intercourse corresponding to these, up to its furthest forms. [10]

Marx and Engels conclude this passage by noting, famously, that ideology too is directly *interwoven with material activity*, although, unlike ideas and conceptions per se, (ruling class) ideology makes 'men and their relations appear upside-down as in a *camera obscura*'.[11] This critique of ideology is something that we have already looked at in some detail, and I would here instead like to draw attention to the dialectic of mental production as proposed in this passage. There is, in the first instance, a division between *mental production* (of ideas, conceptions and also, clearly, of art) on the one hand, and *the mental intercourse of men* on the other. While the latter might be seen as a passive phenomenon (a mere *efflux* of social relations), the former is the scene of emphatically *real, active* engagement. Indeed, if mental production was passive like mental intercourse, then it would (re)produce nothing but ideology. And if our initial (passive) vision of the world is the distorted or *inverted* image that we receive via the dominant ideology of our societies – which, in yet another wonderful analogy, Marx and Engels liken to 'the inversion of objects on the retina'[12] – then we could say that the purpose of mental production is to *uninvert* what we perceive. And to do so, in the same way that physical producers use inorganic material (e.g., as stonecutters use stone), mental producers must use, alter and transform ideological and spiritual materials into works of art.

An explicit account of the relation between artists and the inorganic material that becomes the subject of their labour can be found in the pivotal passage regarding artistic production which I omitted from my earlier discussion of the *Grundrisse*. The particular kind of ideology or spirituality *against and out of which* artists like Homer produced their *eternally charming* poetry was ancient Greek mythology, and after noting that 'Greek mythology is not only the arsenal of Greek art but also its foundation',[13] Marx, writes:

Greek art presupposes Greek mythology, i.e., nature and the
social forms already reworked in an unconsciously artistic way
by the popular imagination. This is its material. Not any mythology whatever, i.e., not an arbitrarily chosen unconsciously
artistic reworking of nature (here meaning everything objective
hence including society). Egyptian mythology could never have
been the foundation or the womb of Greek art. But, in any
case, a *mythology*.[14]

Here Marx again makes a dialectical division between, on the
one hand, (the production of) art – a *nonarbitrary* and *conscious*
use of mythology as *its material* – and, on the other hand, the
objective (or inorganic) *nature* of Greek mythology. Mythology is,
interestingly, itself described as *nature reworked in an unconsciously artistic way by the popular imagination*, but this reworking is not art as such. We might indeed describe the icons, rituals
and relics associated with mythology (or of religions or of all ideologies) as *artistic* or *creative*, but they lack the work or labour of a
real, active and *conscious* producer. We might then say that mythologies have (quasi)artistic aesthetics, but they are not works of
art. Mythology may be described as a more advanced stage of
spirituality, or it can be said to be spirituality aestheticized by
popular imagination – and yet neither spirituality nor mythology is
an art but only art's *material*. Art is concretely different to and yet
dependent on mythology/spirituality/ideology as a baby is vis-à-vis
the *womb*. To extend this metaphor to its fullest semantic capacity, we might say that art is born out of the tenebrous but fertile
space of ideology – or of *the mental intercourse of men apropos
nature* – and that it grows, with the same drive and urgency as that
of an incipient lifeform, until it can no longer be contained in the
womb and must be cut off from the zone of its conception and
incubation and reach a kind of consciousness, capable of ideas,
truths, theories and understanding and, yes, also charm and beauty.
    Since this metaphor and the discussion around it may seem
rather abstract – and potentially *speculative* – I would like to sup-

plement this theory of art with what I hope will be a cogent illustration of Marx's own example of the Homeric epics. For many modern – and ancient – readers of the texts and listeners to oral recitations of them, the *Iliad* and the *Odyssey* have offered the definitive mythological accounts of the Trojan wars and Odysseus's ordeals. It is important to remember, however, that the mythos, gods, goddesses, demi-gods, monsters, and so on that form the content of the poems preexisted their composition, and that Homer's take on them is at odds with many other versions of the same myths. It is also important to emphasize that, while for a modern reader like Marx the poems may offer a kind of enjoyment at the expense of their original milieu's *naïveté*, for the ancient Greek producers and recipients of these poems ('Homer' or whoever their author or authors were, the many performers of the poems, their audiences, etc.) a belief in the power of the mythological figures was far from naïve. Goddess Athena, for example, was not only a fictional figure of a literary narrative, but (for many a believer in her cult) she was also the supernatural or spiritual foundation of city-states such as Athens. The cult of Pallas Athena, both as the city's past matron and its present and future protector, would have arisen in the same way that a belief in hunting or vegetation deities would have come about in earlier, nonurban communities, in tandem with the Athenians' consciousness of their city's development beyond the parameters of a settlement (by the sixth century BCE), of their community acquiring an inorganic objectivity – as *a city* – and exerting a powerful environmental influence – as a post-tribal, protonational economic, social and political milieu – over its inhabitants. The cult of the goddess would have possessed the same ideological powers that existed apropos future religions and secular hegemonic belief systems. The temple dedicated to her dominated the city from the Acropolis, and the wily oligarchs and tyrants, vying for power over the supposedly *democratic* city, never failed to evoke the goddess (often with the collusion of the high priestesses of the goddess's temple) to authorize and justify their might.

We can therefore say that, based on this summary of the cult of Pallas Athena, the ordinary Athenians (be they male citizens, women, youths, slaves or foreigners who lived and worked in the financially burgeoning city) were alienated from the polis's actuality (e.g., its politics) in part due to the authority of and belief in the cult of Athena. And it was not only the devious tyrants who would exploit the image of the goddess to assert their power over the populace – as one tyrant, Peisistratos, once did, by riding into the city in a chariot accompanied by a particularly tall young woman dressed as the goddess – but also self-proclaimed *democrats* such as Pericles, who initiated the construction of the Parthenon, the monumental temple devoted to the goddess. Such political and ideological depictions of the goddess – motifs of a system of the domination of the ruling classes (of Athens' nobility or the so-called *300 families*) over the city, a system that was, if anything, strengthened and not undermined by the advent of Grecian democracy – is starkly different to the way the goddess is shown in a work of art such as the *Odyssey*.

In the poem, she appears as the personal counselor and helper to the struggling hero and, importantly, not as an ostensible, public sign of divine power. At a foundational point in the epic's narrative, Homer's Athena appears in disguise – as a young man – and it is her actions and her personal or intrinsic qualities such as her intelligence, and not the sacred aura of her image and appearance, which assist the hero. The differentiation between Athena as an ideological instrument and her as a figure with intrinsic qualities such as wisdom and loyalty could not be more graphic: in the world of political manipulation and spiritual performance, a real person (the tall Athenian girl) is made to look like Athena by assuming the goddess's emblematic plumed helmet and round shield; but in the work of literary art, Athena is made *intellectually palatable*, deintrumentalized and brought (down) to the level of humanity by shedding her recognizable appearance, that is, her helmet and shield (and, interestingly, her gender with its patriarchal demands for purity, passivity and so on) by assuming instead the form of a *real, active human*. While Homer's Athena remains a deity with (particular and limited) supernatural powers, she is noticeably humanized (subject to anger, joy and vanity) and, more importantly, she enables the human sailor-hero to survive and overcome the properly divine wrath of Poseidon, the god of the sea. We may therefore say that, in the *Odyssey*, and contra the politico-ideological instrumentalizations of Athena in Greek mythology and Athenian society, Athena is produced not as a distant, sublime and awe-inspiring force of nature, but as a very useful figure immediately responsive to the basic needs of the narrative's hero in his fight against the supremacy of a vengeful god.

WHEN WE MAKE ART

What makes a poem like the *Odyssey* something like a timeless masterpiece, then, may be its singular literary qualities – such as the unalienating and memorable characterization of Pallas Athena – and not anything to do with the presumed infancy of Homer's literary milieu. I maintain that Marx's conclusion in the *Grundrisse* regarding the paradox of art's *eternal charm* remains unconvincing, not because I – as a practicing artist in the contemporary ultracapitalist world – cannot but have a personal aversion to accepting his conclusion that 'the unripe social conditions [of openly mythospiritual milieus such as ancient Greece or Elizabethan England] under which [great *flowerings* of art] arose, and could alone arise, can never return'.[15] My observation is that, if art is defined as mental or theoretical use-value produced from mythology and spirituality, then it can continue to be produced out of the raw material of the myths or beliefs of the dominant bourgeois ideologies of our own modern capitalist world.

It may be countered that, by the time of writing of the *Grundrisse*, the mature Marx had abandoned an interest in the theme of ideology altogether, but this supposition would be based on the highly problematic thesis regarding his supposed break with humanism, and it would also ignore that an ideological function, if not ideology per se, can be clearly discerned in the form of the 'metaphysical subtleties and theological niceties'[16] of commodity fetishism in *Capital, Volume One*. Indeed, the assumption that the possibility to produce great art *can never return* in the modern world contradicts Marx's own evaluation of the *splendid* novels of Gaskell and Brontë, and his recommendation of Diderot's *unique masterpiece*. We may now revisit Marx's claim concerning the Victorian novelists' offering us *truths* and agree with him that, seen as transformative reworkings of the myths of modern bourgeois ideology, these novels can indeed be said to produce noninstrumental *social and politics truths* or intrinsic mental use-values. Can they not be seen, therefore, as *a great flowering of art* on par with Homer and Shakespeare?

It is possible to try to resolve this inconsistency in Marx's writing by noting that he did have a personal preference for earlier poetry – for Shakespeare's verse, in particular – as seen in his daughters' recollections of his enthusiastic recitations of what he had memorized of the Bard's poetry. One may also wish to note that the *Grundrisse* is a draft version of Marx's 'economics', not intended for publication as it is, and that, had Marx reconsidered and aimed to publish the work, he may have revised his perspective. Either way, it would be inaccurate and unwarranted to say that for Marx *great* art – which we may now define as an art with a high degree of *intrinsic unalienating mental use-value* – cannot come about under capitalism, particularly if we keep in mind that, despite his disillusionment with the revolutionary movements of the 1840s, and his gradual realization that capital is a far more formidable foe than he may have once imagined it to be, he concludes *Capital, Volume One* by prophesying *a great flowering* of a politics of intrinsic value and truths, when the unchecked power of capitalist *usurpers* brings about their own negation of the negation, and we therefore have 'the expropriation of a few usurpers by the mass of the people'.[17]

Marx does not directly address the topic of art in *Capital, Volume One* , but seeing as we have now defined his theory of art as one premised upon the production of inalienable, universal use-values in the course of concrete mental or theoretical labour, the influential and revealing depictions of use-value production – as opposed to fetishized, capitalist exchange-value accumulation – in his magnum opus may help with further elucidating the process and value of artistic production. In the final section of the first part of the book, for example, he provides an account of the forms of production different to capitalist commodification of labour-power, to highlight 'all the magic and necromancy that surrounds the products of labour' under capitalism, as a result of which the exchange-value of a commodity is no longer rationally measured in accordance with the labour-time expended in the production of the commodity. The first of his examples is both from a work of literature and, I suggest, a demonstration of the kind of unalienating use-value entailed in the process of concrete artistic production:

> Since Robinson Crusoe's experiences are a favourite theme with political economists, let us take a look at him on his island. Moderate though he be, yet some few wants he has to satisfy, and must therefore do a little useful work of various sorts, such as making tools and furniture, taming goats, fishing and hunting. Of his prayers and the like we take no account, since they are a source of pleasure to him, and he looks upon them as so much recreation. In spite of the variety of his work, he knows that his labour, whatever its form, is but the activity of one and the same Robinson, and that it consists of nothing but different modes of human labour. Necessity itself compels him to apportion his time accurately between his different kinds of work. Whether one kind occupies a greater space in his general activity than another, depends on the difficulties, greater or less as the case may be, to be overcome in attaining the useful effect aimed at. This our friend Robinson soon learns by experience, and having rescued a watch, ledger, and pen and ink from the wreck, commences, like a true-born Briton, to keep a set of books. His stock-book contains a list of the objects of utility that belong to him, of the operations necessary for their production; and lastly of the labour-time that definite quantities of those objects have, on average, cost him. All the relations be-

tween Robinson and the objects that form this wealth of his own creation are here so simple and clear as to be intelligible without exertion. . . . And yet those relations contain all that is essential to the determination of value. [18]

It would be tempting to read this passage as a dismissal of the labour value of art, since Robinson's *prayers and the like* are not included alongside the laboured activities conducted for producing use-values. But, as I've already argued, the Marxian notion of art, despite depicting religion and spirituality (and ideology, more generally) as the raw material which artists work with and transform, does not present art itself as *prayers and the like*. Indeed, there is a marked difference in the above passage between *recreation* and *creation*. The former, associated with spirituality and simple *pleasures*, is not seen as *useful work*, even though it is clearly a kind of activity and requires a certain amount of time to perform. *We take no account* of Robinson's prayers in the context of an elucidation of nonfetishistic concrete or immediately useful human labour because in the process of praying (as such) Robinson *does not produce or transform anything* (in the same way that he would by making tools, taming goats, etc.) and merely *looks upon* – or passively consumes – the existing inorganic sources of his (religious) consciousness without actively producing something (new and artistic) out of that consciousness. On the other hand, Marx clearly identifies *creation* as the very heart of productivity and material existence; and if, as I've argued throughout this book through Marx himself, artistic creation is a form of production (albeit of the mental and nonphysical kind) then it too contributes towards the satisfaction of the subject's *few wants*, produces *useful effects* and, finally, has *determinable value*.

Drawing on Marx's earlier, pre-*Capital* writings, we may interpret this important passage from *Capital, Volume One* by making the following observations. First, the *wants* that art satisfies are the mental needs of human subjects that seek to integrate themselves with the world from which they have become consciously alienated, or a world that, to their minds, 'antagonistically confronts'[19] them. Therefore, the usefulness of the art that is produced to satisfy this need may be discerned – and even qualitatively measured if not *judged* in a strict Kantian sense – in the mental or theoretical *utility* or *effects* or capacity of this art in confronting the subjects' (ideologically and spiritually situated) perception of being opposed by an incomprehensible, antagonistic world. Secondly, the value of this activity is related to the level of *difficulty, greater or less as the case may be,* with which that work has been produced; and, finally, art's value may be deemed *determinable* when we take into consideration the amount of time *apportioned* to or taken up by the production of a particular work of art alongside that work's unalienating benefits and uses and the quality (or difficulty) of work carried out in its production. This evaluation of art is clearly not an instrumentalization – even if the word *utility* has been used in this description – as it does not seek to do with art anything other than that for which it was produced originally, that is, the basic satisfaction of a mental need; and, importantly, it is premised – unlike, say, an Aristotelian theory of artistic value – *not* solely on the *effects* of the objects of art (which for Marx, also contra Aristotle, are much more cognitive than affective) but on the genesis of art's value in the milieu of production – in, for example, *the relation* between the time taken to produce the work and the work's effects – and not in the (abstract, ideological, fetishistic) realm of its consumption.

A labour theory of artistic value – unlike, say, a consumeristic or aesthetic theory of artistic value – must take into consideration key material factors, such as the level of complexity or difficulty of the work produced, or the amount of time it has taken an artist to produce a given work, quantifications which would not determine but contribute to the determination of an artwork's value, and which, in the absence of something like Robinson Crusoe's ledger accompanying each work of art, may be discerned in the materiality of the work of art, in, for example, the complexity, scale and skillfulness of the work's execution. Art's value, then, can be arrived at when we consider its mental or theoretical use-value – in giving us truths that counter the obscurities of our ideologies –

alongside and not independently of the level and quantity of labour included in the artistic labour-process. We may therefore add to our previous definition of *great art* that such an art's high level of unalienating use-value is relative to the amount of time and the intensity of artistic labour concentrated in its manifestation.

Marx's fuller conceptualization of concrete labour-process comes relatively late in *Capital, Volume One*, in the book's third part, after much theorization apropos commodification, money and the transformation of money into capital, and it is perhaps one of the notoriously difficult book's challenges that what would seem like a more initial or primordial aspect of human labour is discussed after the rather dense elaboration of the drive and machination for its distortion and exploitation. This strikes me as a sequence akin to meeting a monster or a villain in a gothic or crime narrative prior to meeting and developing sympathy for that antagonist's primary victim. Whatever the reasoning behind the potentially counterinitiative structure of Marx's grand composition, the analysis of the labour-process herein confirms, once and for all, the untenability of the perception of Marx's supposed antihumanism, and also provides us with a more detailed description of production which could further illuminate an understanding of art as labour. He writes:

> Labour is, in the first place, a process in which both man and Nature participate, and in which man of his own accord starts, regulates and controls the material re-actions between himself and Nature. He opposes himself in Nature as one of her own forces, setting in motion arms and legs, head and hands, the natural forces of his body, in order to appropriate Nature's production in a form adapted to his own wants. By thus acting on the external world and changing it, he at the same time changes his own nature. He develops his slumbering powers and compels them to act in obedience to his sway.[20]

This is, in many ways, a more succinct, ripened and sophisticated version of the theory of concrete labour formulated more than twenty years earlier in Paris. Humans produce things that satisfy their needs out of nature, not by *appropriating* nature's resources – as many an environmentalist may think and admonish – but by *appropriating nature's production*, that is, by *becoming productive like nature*, deploying their own natural or biological components (arms, legs, brains, etc.) not to exploit nature or to extract what they want from nature (as, say, a capitalist does vis-à-vis workers' labour-power) but to *compel* the humans' *own* natural powers into working with nature to meet their needs. While I have argued against a perception of Marx as an antihumanist, it should also be clear by now that he is no (ultra-)humanist proponent of anthropocentrism, speciesism and the like. He clearly identifies humans' engagements with nature in the course of the production of intrinsic use-values as a process in which humans participate as *one of nature's own forces*. Despite the undeniably deleterious effects of the actually exploitative modes of production and consumption on the natural environment (e.g., industrial capitalism), and despite the beliefs of the opponents of humanism in our own time, there is nothing in our basic humanity that is intrinsically destructive towards the natural world, or at least not according to Marx's labour theory.

In terms of art, and put in the parlance of artistic production, we can say that here Marx is proposing that, by developing our *slumbering powers* of artistic production in opposition to the *external world* of an alienated consciousness, of myths and ideology, we *change* this world – as in Homer's changing of the sacred Athena into a humanized character of a profane struggle in the *Odyssey* – and, by making such works of art, we *change our own nature* or our own pre-artistic, abject and alienated consciousness. We discover that we ourselves are *one of ideology's own forces*, that ideology and divinity are not powers beyond our ability to challenge or transform but, finally, our own creations, and hence, subjects for new and more truthful and unalienating creations. Marx was more cognizant than most people of his own or any other modern era when it came to the powers and brutality of capital and capitalism, and he was never in denial of the enormous mutilations of the processes by which we make things to live on, disfigurements ushered in and institutionalized by the capitalist ruling classes and their ideologies. He was, in short, anything but naïve when it came to assessing the enormity of the task of changing the world. And yet he has also given us a theory for art's *slumbering powers* to *act on the world and change it*. This theory is, for me, the most compelling view on art's true, intrinsic value proposed by a modern thinker.

NOTES

1. Marx, *Capital*, ed. David McLellan (Oxford: Oxford University Press, 2008), 47.
2. Marx, *Economic and Philosophic Manuscripts of 1844*, trans. Martin Milligan (Moscow: Progress Publishers, 1967), 66.
3. Ibid.
4. Ibid, 96.
5. Ibid.
6. Ibid, 69.
7. Ibid, 70.
8. Marx, *Theories of Surplus Value*, trans. G. A. Bonner and Emile Burns (London: Lawrence & Wishart, 1951), 186.
9. Ibid.
10. Marx and Engels, *The German Ideology, including Theses on Feuerbach and Introduction to the Critique of Political Economy* (New York: Prometheus Books, 1998), 42.
11. Ibid.
12. Ibid.
13. Marx, *Grundrisse: Foundations of the Critique of Political Economy*, trans. Martin Nicolaus (London: Penguin Books, 1993), 110.
14. Ibid.
15. Ibid, 111.
16. Marx, *Capital*, 42.
17. Ibid, 380.
18. Ibid, 47.
19. Marx, *Economic and Philosophic Manuscripts*, 98.

20. Marx, *Capital*, 115.

CONCLUSION
What Is to Be Done (About Art)?

GOODBYE, MARX

By the time of the publication of *Capital, Volume One*, Marx's personal and material circumstances had somewhat improved. An inheritance in 1964 meant that he had moved his family to a London residence more suited to the needs of his three daughters, the oldest of whom, Jenny Caroline or 'Jennychen', was now a young woman of twenty. That same year, and after some initial reluctance, he returned to political activity by joining the General Council of a cross-national amalgam of socialist, communist, trade unionist, anarchist and workerist groups and individuals calling themselves the International Workingmen's Association. Contrary to his own and his comrades' hopes, however, *Capital, Volume One* attracted very little attention upon its publication and its miniscule sales also did very little to help Marx with meeting the costs of educating and marrying his daughters, the second youngest of whom, Laura, was married the year after the publication of her father's complex, complicated masterpiece. Luckily for Marx and his family, Engels was bought out of his father's lucrative cotton mill the following year, and the unfailingly supportive 'General' Engels allocated an annual stipend to his closest friend, 'the Moor'. At last relieved of the burdens of both completing the first volume of his 'economics' and worrying about his personal economic state, Marx, at fifty years of age, was now able to devote himself to organizing a movement that would actively participate in putting an end to *the expropriation by a few usurpers* by cultivating and organizing the power of *the mass of the people*.

Due to the enormous pressures placed on the working people employed by rapidly growing industries, a series of economic crises resulting from overproduction by these industries, and the resurgence in popular anti-imperial militancy in parts of Europe, the International Workingmen's Association was initially quite successful in attracting support and membership; and since, for the time being, its stated aims – carefully articulated by a more mature, more cautious Marx – were not to topple governments but to use legal means such as strikes to gradually further working people's interests within the existing parliamentary parameters of European polities, the organization was not proscribed by the various governments. The outbreak of the Franco-Prussian war of 1870 tested the bonds between the International's French and German members, but it was the unexpected revolutionary upheaval in a Paris battered and humiliated by the triumphant Prussians which proved far more pivotal in terms of the International's fortunes. Although the Paris Commune included very few leaders who were associated with the International, in the immediate aftermath of the greatest threat to the hegemony of the bourgeois ruling classes in close to a century, it was Marx and his politically humble organization which were held partially responsible for ordinary working- and lower-class Parisians' shocking decision to take up arms, assume government control over the French capital, declare *a dictatorship of the proletariat* and be subjected to an extraordinarily brutal suppression by the French state. This was in part due to the publication of what would become the most successful of Marx's works published during his lifetime, a pamphlet passionately defending the defeated Communards, *The Civil War in France*.

This work includes, as we have seen, a vivid description of the bourgeois Parisians' view of the uprising as a macabre spectacle, and shows Marx's continued understanding of art's entanglements with the dramas of war and politics. Marx's own involvement with the event, minimal as it was, would result in his at long last attracting significant public attention. Having been depicted in mainstream newspapers across the Western world as one of the instigators of the Paris Commune, he became the subject of fierce rivalry and antagonism from another key figure in the International, the Russian anarchist Mikhail Bakunin. The tensions between Marx and Bakunin resulted in an open factional war, culminating in Marx and his followers' bid to relocate the General Council to New York in 1872, a move aimed at minimizing Bakunin's influence by taking advantage of what Marx had perceived as support from the readers of his past columns in the *New-York Daily Tribune*. But such a support did not materialize, and Marx would eventually withdraw from engaging with the organization. The International – which would later be dubbed the First International – dissolved in 1876. Marx maintained a level of engagement with politics, particularly by writing to and advising – and at times severely criticizing – the leaders of the newly formed socialist political party in the newly unified Germany, the Socialist Democratic Party of Germany – forerunners to today's Social Democratic Party of Germany (SPD). But Marx's worsening health and the need to seek treatment for his various ailments would prevent him from further publishing or directly participating in political activity. The final years of his life were taken up by his frantic attempts at assisting his daughters with their exceedingly difficult lives, chronic grief over the deaths of his wife and his oldest daughter, prior to his own death, in his sleep, in London at the age of sixty-five.

ART AND THE MARXIST THEORIST

Marx's afterlife has been, arguably, the most significant and the most contested of any philosopher's. Despite their notorious intri-

cacy, density and inaccessibility, his writings on politics, economics and society were turned (by self-proclaimed *Marxists*) into a
series of doctrines that inspired historical upheavals more universally transformative and impactful than anything associated with
the work of any other philosopher in history. (Unless we were to
categorize the Buddha, Jesus and Mohammad as philosophers.)
There is, arguably, very little in Marx's writings that would make
for a readymade program for winning and running government,
but this dearth did not prevent countless radicals from theorizing
about politics, the law, warfare and economic management from a
Marxian perspective. And, on par with the Marxist revolutionaries'
experiments with new forms of insurrection and organization from
Russia to Cuba, from Vietnam to Namibia, Marxist intellectuals
formulated theories and treaties on art that accompanied, anticipated and declared allegiance to a Marxist revolutionary project.

This book has been, in many ways, a participant in this tradition. I remain firm in my view that Marx's theory of art, insofar as I
understand it and am capable of articulating my understanding of
it, is a theory on par with the other major philosophical interventions, from Plato onwards, in the Western understanding of art,
and that Marx's is a highly cogent and compelling account of what
art is and what makes it valuable. I also admit, however, that it was
my original interest in Marx as a thinker of radical change and as
capitalism's most effective adversary that drew me to considering
him in the context of addressing the dilemma of art's value. This
investigation has not, I hope, been overshadowed by my personal
attraction to the revolutionary dimension of Marx's philosophy. I
am, of course, in no denial about the many catastrophic failures of
political Marxism in the twentieth century, but I remain convinced
that these obsessively recounted failures (and the forgotten suc-
cesses, too) are not the direct outcomes of Marx's thoughts per
se – the thoughts of a challenging, difficult poet-cum-philosopher-
cum-journalist who could never have envisaged let alone formulated anything like a straightforward political program for future societies. It is for this reason that my methodology in writing this
book, and the basis for my analyses of Marx's writings on art, has

been to refer only to Marx's own writings and not to those of his many interpreters and critics who have drawn on his writings to offer their own theories. A fresh return to Marx's own primary comments on art have, I hope, helped with obviating the imperative to account for, respond to and incessantly reaffirm or negate the assumptions and consequences of countless thinkers whose oeuvres constitute, directly or otherwise, a rather unwieldy and at times inconsistent system of thought referred to as *Marxist theory*.

That said, I would like to conclude this book, prior to offering some personal reflections on the theory of art as the production of concrete mental use-value, by briefly surveying the artistic theories of key self-identified Marxists and exploring the rapport between their thoughts and Marx's own. In the course of this survey, I will also revisit the three key contemporary philosophers of art with whom I started the book – Badiou, Agamben and Rancière – and reconsider their formulations of art's value in the light of what I've deduced from Marx's philosophy. My aim here is not at all to indulge in the sadly enduring culture of *Marxists-denouncing-fellow-Marxists-for-being-bad-Marxists* – a culture which, despite the universal condemnation of the barbarities of Stalinism, remains in place in the greatly diminished albeit heavily guarded spaces of *Western Marxism, critical theory* and *social justice activism* – but to acknowledge the diverse ways in which Marx's thoughts have been rearticulated, expanded and, in some cases, misrepresented. While it is not at all my intention to be unduly disputatious, it is also an aim of my study to motivate new approaches to Marx's thinking which do not repeat what I see as simplifications and misapplications of Marx's insights.

Due to the limitations imposed by the space available to me in this concluding part of my study, I will only be able to note a very small number of theorists. The first and foremost thinker to note here would have to be the Soviet philosopher Mikhail Lifshitz whose *The Philosophy of Art of Karl Marx* (1933) has been a direct inspiration for my own study and is the only other book-length study of Marx's thoughts on art that I am aware of. In agreement with what I see as Marx's core theory of artistic production, Lifshitz notes, rather briefly, that producing art is 'one of the ways of assimilating nature'.[1] This is not, however, a theme that Lifshitz treats with any prominence – one is tempted to perceive, perhaps unfairly, that Lifshitz's rather tokenistic mention of this theme may be due to what Boris Groys has described as Soviet art's 'project to overcome nature'[2] – and Lifshitz becomes instead rather engrossed in the topic of 'the decadence of art under capitalism'[3] and concludes that 'only communism creates conditions for the growth of culture and art compared to which the limited opportunities that the slaves' democracy offers to a privileged few must necessarily seem meagre'.[4] This interpretation is grounded in an unquestioning reading of the significant passage form the *Grundrisse*, and is perhaps also motivated by a desire to aggrandize the experience of artistic production under Soviet communism. As problematic as both these aspects of Lifshtiz's theory are, I find his depiction of artistic work in our Western democracies as *an opportunity offered to a privileged few* not at all inaccurate.

Georg Lukács, another central Marxist theorist of the same period and an associate of Lifshitz, is much more optimistic about the possibilities of art and literature in *the slaves' democracies* of the West, and champions, in one of his central writings on art, the 1938 essay titled 'Realism in the Balance,' a *'true realist'* such as Thomas Mann in a way that is not dissimilar to Marx's admiration for Dickens and Gaskell.[5] Lukács, however, claims that Dickens and other nineteenth-century novelists made certain 'mistakes' in their representations of social reality because they had written like 'a social scientist would', whereas Mann is a 'creative realist' who 'knows how thoughts and feelings grow out of the life of society and how experiences and emotions are parts of the total complex of reality'.[6] I suspect that a young Marx would take as much issue with this characterization of Mann as he did with a Young Hegelian's praise for the novel *The Mysteries of Paris* which, as we have seen, also posited a predetermined speculative concept of totality as the rubric for the critic's appreciation of the novelist's mastery of a knowledge of this *mystery* of the modern world. That said, Lukács's claim, later in the same essay, contra the pretensions of the modernists, that if 'the surface of life is only experienced immediately, it remains opaque, fragmentary, chaotic and uncomprehended'[7] resonates strongly with Marx's conception of alienation.

Walter Benjamin's 1934 paper 'The Author as Producer' provides an equally Marxian defense of modernism in art, by praising the practice of the experimental photographer who, by fusing text with the photograph, 'wrenches it from modish commerce and gives it a revolutionary useful value'.[8] This essay of Benjamin's is one of the only other works of Marxist theory – other than my own study – which stresses the use-value of art. Against crude Marxist readings (which, perhaps after a narrow adherence to Lukács, remain preoccupied with the *representations* of class and society – and race, gender, etc. – in fiction and the like), Benjamin emphasizes that what matters in an evaluation of art is not the work of art's 'revolutionary themes'[9] or its 'politically correct'[10] tendency – 'astonishing quantities' of which can actually be found in 'the bourgeois apparatus of production'[11] – but the radicalization of the 'processes of production'[12] – as seen in new and 'improved'[13] artistic techniques of modernists such as Bertolt Brecht – who 'adapt'[14] the 'productive apparatus' (e.g., a literary genre or a theatrical device) 'to the purposes of the proletarian revolution'.[15] Like Marx himself, Benjamin derides the submission of art to ideology – even supposedly *revolutionary* or *politically correct* ideology – and dismisses art's 'value as propaganda'[16] in favor of the work's inventive artistic qualities. That said, Benjamin's enthusiasm for some modernist art's – for example, Brechtian theatre's – penchant for 'alienating' the audience (even if this is an alienation from the alienation of life in capitalist society)[17] strikes me as rather questionable, and one is left wondering how any kind of alienation (with its resulting confusion, fear and ignorance) may be seen as *useful improvement*.

Benjamin's fellow Frankfurt school thinker Theodor Adorno's development of an explicitly Marxian approach to the question of art is at its clearest in some of the fragments that comprise *Minima Moralia* (1951). Adorno intensifies the view of art's degradation under capitalism by depicting the contemporary as a milieu in which the (Idealist) separation between the fine and the mechanical is revealed excessively, and this excess threatens the very status of art. Adorno claims that, traditionally, the work of art has sought to 'silence' 'the fatal question' regarding the work's mechanical genesis – to 'eradicate the traces of making' – via the appearance of the work as something associated with genius or 'perfection'.[18] But capitalist modes of production – the models of which are 'syntactically concocted by film and hit-song for the bleak contemplation of the late industrial era' – 'liquidate art' by laying bare the work of art's material basis and exposing its claims to perfection as a 'delusion.'[19] While Adorno has come to a somewhat similar conclusion to Marx regarding art's plight under capitalism, he has come to this view via accepting a (Kantian) division between perception (of genius) and (*mere* physical) production, a division that is of course undermined by Marx's radical belief in the producibility of perception. Later on, however, Adorno moves significantly closer to Marx, by suggesting that some aesthetically produced objects – such as toys and marionettes – can evoke (at least for the child) 'the joy of doing'[20] and allow the child to side 'with use-value against exchange value.'[21] Adorno hesitates to ascribe such a capacity to the work of art as such – mired, as it is, in the *bleakness* of culture-industrial reifications and so on – but he detects 'colourful and useful'[22] images such as those that constitute a child's view of the world – a view that is 'purified of appropriation'[23] by capitalists and their false 'mediated usefulness'[24] – in artistic products such as fairytales and operettas.[25]

Adorno arrives at this observation by reflecting on 'life's magic'[26] – after the poet Hebbel – in something of an agreement with Benjamin's view of magic as a key dimension of early art, an understanding that forms the basis of Ernest Fischer's important book-length study of art from a Marxian perspective, *The Necessity of Art* (1959). Fischer claims, after Benjamin, that 'art in its origin was *magic*'[27] ; however, contra Benjamin and after Marx, Fischer does not hold a salutary view of (any kind of) alienation, and he therefore redefines magic not as a kind of alienation or ideology, but as 'an aid towards mastering a real but unexplored world.'[28] He goes as far as to claim that in magic 'religion, science and art were combined in a latent form'.[29] Cautious as Fischer is in associating art (and science) with religion – by saying that their supposed combination is *latent* – it seems frankly impossible to envisage, from a Marxian perspective, any kind or degree of fusion between the dialectically divided mental *intercourse* of (religious) ideology, on the one hand, and the mental *productions* of art (and science) on the other. To perhaps compensate for this problem, and to also provide an interpretation of Marx's view of art in the *Grundrisse*, Fischer suggests that 'the magic role of art' is something that has been eroded with the historical development of the modes of production, and that art is no longer 'bound by the rigid forms of the earlier ages where the magic element still operated'.[30] This move allows Fischer to not only rescue art from magic's alienating imperative, but to also appreciate – contra Marx's own excessively and unnecessarily negative view, in the *Grundrisse*, of art in the modern world – 'more open forms' of modern art such as the novel, which, despite its radically different form, content and techniques vis-à-vis ancient poetry, has a role or a use-value similar to that of ancient art, in 'helping men to recognize and change social reality'.[31]

Hebert Marcuse tries a 'reconciliation' between what he sees as art's useful capacity to intensify alienation – for him, as with many other Frankfurt school Marxists (e.g., Benjamin), 'art is committed to that perception of the world which alienates individuals from their functional existence and performance in society'[32] – with 'strong affirmative tendencies'[33] in his 1977 pamphlet *The Aesthetic Dimension*. While Marcuse uses (his positive depiction of) artistic alienation to counter what he sees as the 'devastating consequences' of a 'normative'[34] Lukácsian valorization of realism, he thinks, unlike many modernists, that art must also embody 'the power of recognition which gives the individual a modicum of freedom and fulfillment.'[35] This synthesis of *alienation-and-recognition* does address what I noted earlier as Benjamin's problematic ebullience for the alienating quality of Brecht's *epic theatre*; however, Marcuse's solution in the form of catharsis and 'the power of the aesthetic'[36] does not seem very convincing. I agree with Marcuse that Marx's attempt at explaining away ancient Greek art's *eternal charm* by resorting to an image of *the childhood of humanity* is 'hardly persuasive',[37] but I also maintain that the (Aristotelian) cathartic values of delight, pleasure and purification of emotions are not intrinsic to use-value production, but are found in the space of exchange-value consumption. Marcuse's proposal that art's affirmative potential is found in the sensual pleasures associated with the supposed 'commitment of art to Eros'[38] may have more to do with the liberal *progressive* ideologies and cultural particularities of Marcuse's *countercultural* milieu – and its desire for sexual liberation from 'social oppression'[39] – than a reflection on Marx's original view of art and its intrinsic uses.

A far more convincing Marxian take on art comes from, somewhat unexpectedly, none other than the originator of what I've referred to, throughout this book, as an unpersuasive view of Marx's antihumanism. While I disagree with Louis Althusser's thesis apropos an *epistemological break*, I believe that Marx's philosophy does dramatically deviate from, but does not irrevocably break with, previous (Aristotelian, Cartesian and Idealist) versions of humanism. (And I will gladly state, if need be, that in my view humanism is not an undesirable, expired project, and that it remains a powerful intellectual resource even in our era of up-to-the-minute *posthumanism* and widespread ideological dread apropos the so-called anthropocene.) There exists, at any rate, a terrific articulation of Marx's view of the relationship between art and ideology in one of Althusser's letters, written in response to a literary scholar called André Daspre, first published in the journal *La Nouvelle Critique* in 1966. In what expands and elucidates Marx's depiction of ancient Greek poetry as conceived in *the womb* of Greek mythology, Althusser writes that ideology is that 'from which [art] is born, in which it bathes, from which it detaches itself as art, and which it *alludes*'.[40]

Art, according to this formulation, has a nonhuman autonomy or objectivity – *it detaches itself*, without, seemingly, the intervention of an artist/ic midwife – which may be difficult to envisage, particularly in the light of Marx's persistent attentiveness (from his juvenile poems to *Capital*) to the concrete human labour of art, and his view of art as something mentally produced by *real, active* people. Nevertheless, Althusser seems justified to weaken the role of the artist in keeping with Marx's own attacks on the Young Hegelians' idealized obsessions with *geniuses* and *born-poets* and the like – although I maintain that a complete erasure of the role of the artist or of the human producer would be very much consonant with the ultracapitalist or neoliberal drive for abstracting, minimizing and marginalizing labourers to better exploit their labour-power. At any rate, Althusser's view of the work of art as something detached from ideology (irrespective of who or what performs the detachment, the work or the worker) which continues to *allude* to its ideology – in the same way that we might say a child may be similar to but not identical to his or her parents – provides a succinct and memorable image of art's relationship with ideology. A child belongs to the same species as her mother – and ideology and art too are members of *the same nonphysical or mental species* – and she may even look like her mother or share some traits with her mother, but she is simply not the same person as her mother. Art too, therefore, may refer to – even be said to partially represent – the social reality in which it is born (as Lukács may have it) and perhaps even share some of the alienating traits of this reality (as Benjamin may have it), but it is neither a representation (e.g., a clone) of reality, nor an objectivation of its forces of alienation. It is, simply, not the same thing as ideology.

Australian scholar Pauline Johnson, in her 1984 book *Marxist Aesthetics* (which bears the telling subtitle: *The Foundations Within Everyday Life for an Emancipated Consciousness*), observes that Althusser's 'inability to give an account of the foundations [of art] in immediate experience'[41] prevents him from offering an account of art which does indeed detach it from ideology. According to her, since ideology can only be known to us via consciousness (which Marx would basically agree with) and consciousness is premised upon experience (which Marx would only partially agree with), therefore a theory such as Althusser's which undervalues experience cannot contribute towards an artistic transformation of ideology. She labels Althusser – and many of the preceding Marxist theorists – 'cultural aristocrats'[42] for their dismissal of the validity of a (semi-Kantian) appreciation of quotidian aesthetic experience. She, however, also rejects the temptations of the postmodern and derides 'the false democracy of a radical populist alternative' and its 'attempt to locate a nascent resistant consciousness within a variety of popular culture practices.'[43] While highly critical of previous Marxists, she recognizes that 'the tradition of Marxist aesthetics has consistently *attempted* to articulate and to work through the vital problem of the possibility within the present for effective ideological change.'[44] As for her own vision of such a possibility, and when not preoccupied with critiquing past critics, she advocates 'a conception grounded in an analysis of felt, radical needs.'[45] While Johnson's insistent attacks on the supposed 'insidious, covert elitism'[46] of Marxist thinkers are less than convincing and lack a socioeconomic concept of elitism – and may label an impoverished, exiled Marx himself a dreaded elite due to his love of Homer, Shakespeare and Goethe – Johnson's valorization of fundamental *needs* is very much in keeping with the foundations of Marx's philosophy of art.

Johnson's valuing of what is *felt* is also significant, and consonant with a certain line of Anglophone Marxism associated with Raymond Williams and Terry Eagleton (despite the latter's equally Althusserian influences). And it is with a consideration of Eagleton's articulation of Marx's theory of art, in one of his more recent publications, that I would like to conclude this brief review of Marxist theorists of art. In the 2011 book *Why Marx Was Right*, Eagleton cites Marx's note regarding Milton from *Theories of Surplus-Value* as an example of a kind of 'true production.'[47] For Eagleton, the possibly for people to produce 'freely and for its own sake' may be realized 'only under communism' – and, needless to say, here he is not at all referring to the failed totalitarianisms of the twentieth century which claimed to be communistic – and, until such a realization, 'we can get a foretaste of such creativity in a specialized form of production known as art.'[48] Eagleton speaks very much after Marx when he goes on to declare that 'art is an image of nonalienated labour'[49] ; but one can also sense a degree of theoretical instrumentalization in Eagleton's depiction of art as an *image* that gives us a *foretaste* of something else. Is art – *freely and for its own sake* – creative, nonalienated labour; or does it exist to give us a taste of such a labour and therefore perhaps appetize us for a postalienation future, as a means for a greater, theoretically more desirable end? Eagleton might reply that art can be both things; but, at least as articulated in this text of his, it seems that art is limited to some kind of theoretical hors d'oeuvre, preparing us for the main course that will not be artistic but universal-historic. Neither Marx nor any artist with a serious affiliation to a Marxist intellectual tradition would want art to *not* prepare us for a future of liberation from exploitation and alienation – and such a preparation is, in my view, possible and real – but such a desire can only come after (or, at the very least, be contemporaneous with) the maintenance of art's actual, intrinsic value *for the time being*, irrespective of when – and, hopefully, not *if* – capitalism has run its course and we finally free ourselves of it.

MARX AND THE CONTEMPORARY PHILOSOPHIES OF ART

Finally, I'd like to return to my problematization of the theories of the contemporary philosophers of art and the possibilities for addressing these in the light of my investigation of Marx's theory of artistic value. Badiou, Agamben and Rancière are, in different ways and to varying degrees, part-practitioners of a Marxian philosophical project, despite their obvious, non-Marxian influences and emphases. It would not therefore be extraneous to suggest Marxian additives or even amendments to ameliorate what I've argued to be these philosophers' difficulties in proposing an effective view of art's intrinsic value.

In terms of Badiou's theory of the *inaesthetic*, I have suggested that his proposal – that a work of art produces truths that can either be known via their discernable effects as found in other works of art, as novel originators of *artistic configurations*, or be evaluated in their capacity to rupture the regimes of opinion – does not, as it stands, offer a particularly compelling theory apropos art's immanent and singular, that is, intrinsic value. However, if art is seen, after Marx, as laboured production, and if, therefore – à la Benjamin's development of Marx – artistic innovation is seen as an improvement made to an apparatus of production (and not simply as an act of Romantic *genius* exceptionalism that must, by definition, engender a cultish artistic following, something that, as Kant has observed quite correctly, reduces the *great* work of art to a model to be utilized, imitated and, therefore, instrumentalized by nongreat artists), then it is possible to see Badiou's plea for artistic novelty as an argument for art's value in itself, a value found in the immanent materiality of the work itself, and not in (our knowledge of) the consequences of the event of a specific work's future incorporations into the states of artistic practice.[50] Apropos Badiou's desire to see art as a radical break with public opinion, while this characterization of art already resonates with Marx's view that art produces theoretical use-values contra ideology, Badiou's analysis depends rather strongly on art's capacity to demonstrably oppose a given doxa and runs the risk of reducing art to a tool or a weapon to be utilized (cited, referenced, etc.) by a radical thinker against the conservatism of existing thought. As we have seen, Marx too has used art in not dissimilar ways – in, for instance, his referencing a poem by Goethe to illustrate a truth contra the common perceptions of British colonialism – but, as I've argued, for him a much more primary and noninstrumental understanding of art's mental use-value is found not in art's opposition to ideology per se but in art's transformation of the alienating objects of ideology into unalienating objects of art. As such, Badiou's (obviously Platonic) theory of truth, if articulated more explicitly in terms of an artistic truth's negation of alienation, would place the emphasis back on the work of art itself, on its intrinsically unalienating purpose, and not on its (hoped for) ability to contradict or alter public perceptions.

Agamben's theory of art's value, and its proposal for art's adopting alienation itself as one of its own tropes, is obviously conversant with the Frankfurt school interpretations of Marx's theory of art. As I've noted with regard to these interpretations, however, if, as Marx quite unambiguously states, alienation in the modern world is an ideological tenet of capitalism (found in the ideas of the ruling classes and their *mental intercourse*, and also in the capitalist modes of production, consumption and surplus-value extraction), then alienation is clearly a dimension of abstract, commercial or commodified exchange-value instrumentalization and not (even if seen, however charitably, as a negation of capitalist alienation) conducive to the concrete production of intrinsic use-values. However, if Agamben's proposal for the *adoption* of alienation is radicalized to the point of this adoption becoming a transformation, it may offer concrete methods for liberating art from the *desert of the aesthetic*, instead of fomenting *nostalgic* yearning for the past possibilities of art. In light of Marx's own detailed explications of art's mutilations and disfigurations under capitalism, Agamben may seem justified to resort to a *melancholic* attitude when it comes to art in the contemporary world. Art's use-value, however, cannot be expunged by capitalism since, dialectically, art's intrinsic use-value, as defined in opposition to alienation, cannot but grow in proportion to the growth of capital's scope and scale of alienation itself, and therefore – again, contra Marx's own unpersuasive comment on *the childhood of humanity* in the *Grundrisse* – Agamben's theory could help with approaching an intrinsic value of art if art does not simply mimic capitalist alienation (and both *nostalgia* and *melancholia* strike me as the symptoms of the artist's realization of, precisely as Agamben would have it, art's *inability to leap beyond* merely mocking ruling class ideology) but *reverse* or *undo* or, at the very least, detach itself, after Althusser, from the sources of alienation.

Finally, it might seem that Rancière's theory of art already adheres to some aspect of Marx's philosophy of art as proposed in this book. Rancière, unlike most other thinkers considered in this book, deploys the word *use* in a positive, productive sense – he associates art with the forms that life *uses* to form itself – not so unlike Marx himself; and Rancière's proposal that art could contribute to the *formation of a specific kind of humanity* may be said to echo Marx's own belief in the eventuality of communism and those of his Soviet advocates (such as Lifshitz). Such *uses* and contributions are, however, based on Rancière's perception of the autonomy of the aesthetic, and of art being submissive to this autonomy, or subject to an *aesthetic regime*. This perception both instrumentalizes art – by depicting art as simply a conduit for what can be described as a (Hegelian) *spirit* of an *aesthetic revolution* – and, contemporaneous or perhaps even coterminous with this instrumentalization, it completely ignores Marx's concerns with ideology. For Rancière, the autonomy of the aesthetic is nothing other than an autonomy from ideology, a view which may seem entirely incompatible with a Marxian perspective which sees bourgeois tastes and sensibilities very much complicit with bourgeois ideology and bourgeois modes of production. However, as I've mentioned before, Marx does note the possibility for a concrete aesthetic – as seen in his description of *the five senses as a labour of history* – and should Rancière too account for the ways in which the aesthetic, as labour and not as some kind of given perceptual *gift*, is abstracted and alienated under modern capitalism, then his theory may also be able to demonstrate that art is not merely a tool of the (alienated) aesthetic. If art is something that could have a properly political capacity or a capacity for intervening or at least participating in the *polis* as per Rancière's stated aims – or, frankly, if art is to have any capacity whatsoever, other than making us aware of the power of the aesthetic – then art must be seen, as I've argued after what I understand of Marx's philosophy, as the condition for producing truths or use-values that seek to unalienate and liberate the aesthetic itself.

SO, WHAT'S ART GOOD FOR?

I began this book by citing instances of the discourse of artistic value in contemporary Western capitalist societies and by highlighting the overt emphases given by the most influential participants in this discourse (governmental arts administrators, arts professionals, economists, etc.) to the arts' instrumental values. I noted that these *stakeholders* view art as something that can somehow be utilized to deliver benefits to do with *health and well-being, our individual lives*, or with *stimulating the economy*. It would be quite easy, in light of this investigation of Karl Marx's radical thought, to dismiss this discourse *tout court* as an ideological distortion of the truths of art in tandem with the consciousness and mental intercourse of the technomanagerial ruling elites. But to say that art should therefore only be seen as an intrinsically valuable activity would amount to a kind of Idealism which, as we have seen, would result in its own speculative, moralist and spiritualist instrumentalization. Marx, although never forgoing the primary centrality of concrete use-value production, did not see this intrinsic quality as existing independent from the modes of production, ideation and consumption. I think it would be accurate to say that for Marx, the ruling class build their power on the foundation of exploiting the labour-power of the masses of the people; but, as the modes of production change (from, say, slavery to feudalism) so do the forms of ideology and alienation that accompany them (changing from, for example, mythology to monotheism). The masses of the people, exploited and subjected to the (increasingly more mechanical and inhuman) modes of production and alienation, will respond to this subjection *not by returning to their pre-exploitation humanity* (and not by forgoing their humanity) but *by inventing a new humanity* (e.g., a radicalized bourgeoisie in the seventeenth and eighteenth centuries, or a politicized proletariat in the nineteenth and twentieth centuries) as a result of their pursuit of their primal need for producing things that enable them to live in the world in the contexts of the new and increasingly more alienating modes of technological and mental exploitation.

Marx, in short, would see the relationship between an intrinsic and an instrumental value (or between the exploited and the exploiters, or between labour and capital) as deeply dialectical and symbiotic. It would therefore be erroneous to reject the utilitarianism of the contemporary discourses of art in the name of (an Idealized notion of) art's deeper value. We must instead find art's deeper value as something necessitated by the dynamics and materiality of the dominant ideological discourses themselves. Even though the instinct or the drive to make art is a properly *timeless* human quality, the form and substance of how art is made, the kinds of art that are made, the techniques and the content of the arts, and the concrete uses of making art or art's truths are situated only in the material, cultural and historical contexts of given artistic events. Therefore, a genuine critique of the contemporary perceptions of art and its value must begin with an understanding of these perceptions as ideologies in the strict Marxian sense of the word: as the mental dimension of modes of production that benefit and empower *the few usurpers* at the expense *of the masses of the people*.

An important discussion must be had, I believe, regarding the direct artistic exploiters of our world, and the different degrees of exploitation carried out by groups or individuals in widely uneven positions within the professional or vocational hierarchies. The multibillionaire CEO of an entertainment empire and the underpaid (or, often, unpaid) administrative assistant at a community cultural event are not, economically or socially, equals; but they have both based the procurement of their own (material or mental) interest on the exchange-value of the (artistic, or cultural) products made by people other than themselves. I am obviously not able to advance a discussion on such an intricate topic in these final remarks of the concluding part of this book, a discussion that should avoid a simplistic binary of *makers versus profiteers*, a designation which runs the risk of overlooking the material and historical development and necessities of the divisions of labour in the art industries. It seems, at any rate, correct to say that the discourse of art as something with social benefits (*health, education,* etc.) or with commercial benefits (*revenue streams, returns for future performances*) is one that serves the interests of (groups on widely disparate and unequal levels of) social and commercial bourgeoisie, not the interests of the producers of the works of art. Does this mean that art does not have social and commercial benefits? Certainly not – even Plato, as we have seen, despite his notorious prohibition of the arts, concedes that some arts may have a didactic value – but we should also be aware that an emphasis on art's social and commercial values, as opposed to its intrinsically artistic value, is an expression of the values and interests of those who profit from the artistic production of the others.

What would an expression of a belief in art's intrinsic use-value entail? This book has been an attempt at articulating precisely such an expression. I recognize that my understanding of Marx may be open to criticism – for its passé fidelity to a kind of humanism, for its omission of major Marxist theorists of art (Williams, Bourdieu, Macherey, Jameson, Žižek, etc.) – and that my sympathetic approach to Marx may in itself be deemed suspicious, not only by the *conservatives* who might see Marx as somehow complicit in a diabolical thing called *communist totalitarianism* (and the gulags, etc.) but also by the self-proclaimed *progressive* champions of *identity politics* for whom Marx is, altogether, too White, too European, too male, too heterosexual, and so forth. Nevertheless, I hope that the theory of art as put forward in this book contributes to a greater appreciation of art's value, as something that we make (and have always made and will keep on making) because art can, in entirely unique and differentiated ways, help us confront and overcome the fear and alienation caused by (our own habitual, socially and economically institutioned ignorance of) the world and its nature.

Art can never be an *opium of the masses*. It is an actual activity – that takes time, effort, techniques – that provides us with the understanding that we have been opiated, and that we are complicit in our being drugged and deluded. It is through and as part of this understanding that we make objects (poems, paintings, novels, music) that negate and, at their most potent, rupture our addiction to the opium of religion, in more traditional societies, and our equally destructive, alienating habit of depending on the mythic, unfulfillable dreams and promises of prosperity, endless pleasure and individual success in our modern capitalist societies. We live in a world mentally dominated by a zeitgeist of technoeconomic hubris and misplaced optimisms (in *the new economy, digital revolution, the global village*, and so on) and its corresponding alienating, incapacitating nihilisms (of *global warming, terrorism, the rise of the far-right*) while, precisely as Marx has foreseen, the forces of global capitalist accumulation rapidly and uncontrollably decimate the very class that was once the vanguard of this system of economic domination, the bourgeois middle class, in favor of an unfathomably rich oligarchy, resulting in the most materially unequal society in human history. The work of art can counter the unconscious submission of our consciousness to the ideology of this world, by demonstrating, to the best of the artist's productive ability, that we should neither acquiesce to the diktats of capital nor live in abject fear of them.

The most valuable property of art today may be to insist on the dignity and the potential truthfulness of the human subject, contra the fearsome, inhuman forces of incapacity and alienation that rule our world. A truly revolutionary art may show us how we may become a collective, universal subject, capable of changing the world and its history. Such an art would have a wonderfully true, intrinsic value.

NOTES

1. Mikhail Lifshitz, *The Philosophy of Art of Karl Marx*, trans. Ralph B. Winn (New York: Critics Group, 1938), 65.

2. Boris Groys, *The Total Art of Stalinism: Avant-garde, Aesthetics, Dictatorship, and Beyond*, trans. Charles Rougle (London: Verso, 2011), 126.

3. Lifshitz, 86.

4. Ibid, 94

5. Georg Lukács, 'Realism in the Balance', in Theodor Adorno et al., *Aesthetics and Politics* (London: Verso, 2006), 36.

6. Ibid.

7. Ibid, 39.

8. Walter Benjamin, "The Author as Producer," *Reflections: Essays, Aphorisms, Autobiographical Writings*, trans. Edmund Jephcott (New York: Schocken Books, 2007), 230.

9. Ibid, 229.

10. Ibid, 221.

11. Ibid, 229.

12. Ibid, 230.

13. Ibid, 231.

14. Ibid, 238.

15. Ibid.

16. Ibid, 233.

17. Ibid, 236.

18. Theodor Adorno, *Minima Moralia*, trans. E. F. N. Jephcott (London: Verso, 2005), 226.

19. Ibid.

20. Ibid, 227.

21. Ibid, 228.

22. Ibid, 227.

23. Ibid.

24. Ibid, 228.

25. Ibid.

26. Ibid, 227.

27. Ernst Fischer, *The Necessity of Art*, trans. Anna Bostock (London: Verso, 2010), 22.

28. Ibid.

29. Ibid.

30. Ibid.

31. Ibid.

32. Hebert Marcuse, *The Aesthetic Dimension*, trans. Herbert Marcuse and Erica Sherover, (London: Macmillan, 1979), 9.

33. Ibid, 10.

34. Ibid, 3.

35. Ibid, 10.

36. Ibid.

37. Ibid, 15.

38. Ibid, 11.

39. Ibid.

40. Louis Althusser, *Lenin and Philosophy and Other Essays*, trans. Ben Brewster (New York: Monthly Review Press, 2001), 152.

41. Pauline Johnson, *Marxist Aesthetics: The Foundations Within Everyday Life for an Emancipated Consciousness* (Routledge, 2011); ProQuest Ebook Central, 146.

42. Ibid, 143.

43. Ibid, 148.

44. Ibid, 144.

45. Ibid, 145.

46. Ibid, 148.

47. Terry Eagleton. *Why Marx Was Right* (New Haven: Yale University Press, 2018), 123.

48. Ibid.

49. Ibid.

50. In his most recent philosophical publication – *L'Immanence des vérités* (Paris: Fayard, 2018) – released at the time of the completion of my study, Badiou himself has addressed the problem of 'comment l'œuvre d'art pourtait être évaluée' (28). He acknowledges that, contra the (Kantian) view that 'l'œuvre d'art comparaisse toujours sur fond d'infinité', we must be able to think – or, perhaps indeed, *produce* – our own immanent 'procédures de réinterprtation' (Ibid), but he does not go as far as advocating a more explicitly materialist theory of production. Nevertheless, that the work (*œuvre*) has now seemingly become a key topic of Badiou's philosophy may be seen as a gesture in the direction of resolving the kind of problem that I propose to have found in his theories of artistic evaluation.

FURTHER READING

I maintain, as I have throughout this study, that any investigation of Karl Marx's thinking on art must begin with reading his own writings on art which, as I hope I have demonstrated in this book, are neither meager nor incoherent. Nevertheless, and for those who wish to look beyond the necessarily brief selection of works on art from Marxist perspectives presented in the conclusion, I wish to recommend the following texts which show a variety of approaches to artistic topics by thinkers who have, to varying degrees, subscribed or contributed to Marx's aesthetical project.

Adorno, Theodor, Walter Benjamin, Ernest Bloch, Bertolt Brecht, and Georg Lukács. *Aesthetics and Politics*. London: Verso, 2006. A compilation of exchanges and arguments apropos art and artistic production between several early to mid-twentieth-century Marxist theorists of art.

Ahmad, Aijaz. *In Theory: Classes, Nations, Literatures*. London: Verso, 1992. A polemical defence of a Marxian approach to literature contra the critical fashions of the bourgeois American academe.

Barthes, Roland. *Mythologies*. Translated by Annette Lavers. London: Vintage, 2000. An incisive account of the common artistic and aesthetic phenomena and ephemera of the author's world with an eye to their ideological functions.

Benjamin, Walter. *Illuminations*. Translated by Harry Zohn. London: Fontana Press, 1992. A crucial work of Marxist aesthetics which includes the seminal essay 'The Work of Art in the Age of Mechanical Reproduction'.

Berger, John. *Ways of Seeing*. London: Penguin Books, 1977. An influential and engaging materialist revision of the common themes of visual-artistic perception and appreciation.

Bourdieu, Pierre. *The Field of Cultural Production.* Translated by Randal Johnson. New York: Columbia University Press, 1993. A sociological account of the place of aesthetic production in the milieu of capitalist culture and society.

Debord, Guy. *Society of the Spectacle.* Translated by Ken Knabb. London: Rebel Press, 2011. A highly influential depiction of the capitalist milieu as one utilizing a grand, obfuscating aesthetics to advance hegemonic domination.

Eagleton, Terry. *Marxism and Literary Criticism.* Berkley: University of California Press, 1976. An informative, accessible synthesis and application of a number of Marxist approaches to literature, which has had a lasting impact on the Anglophone approach to Marxist literary theory.

Hall, Stuart, and Paddy Whannel. *The Popular Arts.* Durham, NC: Duke University Press, 2018. A materialist, albeit not particularly dialectical, account of the less overtly artistic products of the cultural spaces under capitalism.

Jameson, Fredric. *The Political Unconscious: Narrative as a Social Symbolic Act.* London: Methuen, 1981. An important attempt at exposing the political ideologies of capitalism as deeply embedded in understated narrative and aesthetic assumptions and practices.

Macherey, Pierre. *A Theory of Literary Production.* Translated by Geoffrey Wall. London: Routledge, 2006. A rigorous investigation of literary works in terms of their relationship with the ideologies and class interests of their authors and their worlds.

Rose, Margaret A. *Marx's Lost Aesthetic: Karl Marx and the Visual Arts.* Cambridge: Cambridge University Press, 1984. A compelling and original account of Marx's thinking on visual arts and its possible affinities with the thought of the earlier socialist Henri de Saint-Simon.

Ross, Kristin. *The Emergence of Social Space: Rimbaud and the Paris Commune.* London: Verso, 2007. A thorough discussion of a number of poems by a specific author, Arthur Rimbaud, from a materialist perspective attuned to Marxian imperatives.

Trotsky, Leon. *Literature and Revolution.* Edited by William Keach. Chicago: Haymarket Books, 2005. A key example of an account of the nature and manifestations of literary arts from the perspective of radical, political Marxism.

Williams, Raymond. *Marxism and Literature.* Toronto: Oxford University Press. 1977. A lucid and systemic construction of the place and particularities of literature from the author's own take on Marx's theory of cultural production.

Wilson, Sarah. *Picasso/Marx and Socialist Realism in France.* Liverpool: Liverpool University Press, 2013. A detailed and engrossing account of a variety of Marxist responses to the work of a particular artist, Pablo Picasso.

Žižek, Slavoj. *The Sublime Object of Ideology.* London: Verso, 1995. A central work by an author who has explored the ideological tropes and messages of artistic and aesthetic phenomena including popular movies and everyday objects.

BIBLIOGRAPHY

Adorno, Theodor. *Minima Moralia*. Translated by E. F. N. Jephcott. London: Verso, 2005.

Adorno, Theodor, Walter Benjamin, Ernest Bloch, Bertolt Brecht, and Georg Lukács. *Aesthetics and Politics*. London: Verso, 2006.

Agamben, Giorgio. *The Man Without Content*. Translated by Georgia Albert. Stanford: Stanford University Press, 1999.

Ahmad, Aijaz. *In Theory: Classes, Nations, Literatures*. London: Verso, 1992.

Althusser, Louis. *Lenin and Philosophy and Other Essays*. Translated by Ben Brewster. New York: Monthly Review Press, 2001.

Aristotle. *Poetics*. Translated by Malcolm Heath. London: Penguin, 1996.

Arts Council England. "The Value of Arts and Culture to People and Society." Arts Council England. Accessed 21 July 2017. http://www.artscouncil.org.uk/exploring-value-arts-and-culture/value-arts-and-culture-people-and-society.

Augustine of Hippo. *Confessions*. Translated by R. S. Pine-Coffin. London: Penguin Books, 1961.

Badiou, Alain. *Handbook of Inaesthetics*. Translated by Alberto Toscano. Stanford: Stanford University Press, 2005.

———. *L'Immanence des vérités*. Paris: Fayard, 2018.

Barthes, Roland. *Mythologies*. Translated by Annette Lavers. London: Vintage, 2000.

Beech, Dave. *Art and Value: Art's Economic Exceptionalism in Classical, Neoclassical and Marxist Economics*. Leiden: Brill, 2015.

Benjamin, Walter. *Illuminations*. Translated by Harry Zohn. London: Fontana Press, 1992.

———. *Reflections: Essays, Aphorisms, Autobiographical Writings*. Translated by Edmund Jephcott. New York: Schocken Books, 2007.

Bennett, Tony. *Formalism and Marxism*. London: Methuen & Co. Ltd., 1979.

Berger, John. *Ways of Seeing*. London: Penguin Books, 1977.

Bourdieu, Pierre. *The Field of Cultural Production*. Translated by Randal Johnson. New York: Columbia University Press, 1993.

Bourriaud, Nicholas. *Relational Aesthetics*. Translated by Simon Pleasance and Fiona Woods. Dijon: Les presses du réel, 2009.

Caruth, Nicole J. "What Is the Value of Art?" *Art21 Magazine*, 28 May 2014. Accessed 21 July 2017. http://magazine.art21.org/2014/05/28/flash-points-what-is-the-value-of-art/.

Debord, Guy. *Society of the Spectacle*. Translated by Ken Knabb. London: Rebel Press, 2011.

Eagleton, Terry. *Marxism and Literary Criticism*. Berkley: University of California Press, 1976.

———. *Why Marx Was Right*. New Haven: Yale University Press, 2018.

Fischer, Ernst. *The Necessity of Art*. Translated by Anna Bostock. London: Verso, 2010.

Groys, Boris. *The Total Art of Stalinism: Avant-garde, Aesthetics, Dictatorship, and Beyond*. Translated by Charles Rougle. London: Verso, 2011.

Hall, Stuart, and Paddy Whannel. *The Popular Arts*. Durham: Duke University Press, 2018.

Hassan, Toni. "How Do You Put a Value on Art, and the People Creating It?" *The Sydney Morning Herald*, 9 March 2016. Accessed 21 July 2017. https://www.smh.com.au/opinion/how-do-you-put-a-value-on-art-and-the-people-creating-it-20160309-gne4sc.html.

Hegel, Georg Wilhelm Friedrich. *Introductory Lectures on Aesthetics*. Translated by Bernard Bonsanquet. London: Penguin, 2004.

Jameson, Fredric. *The Political Unconscious: Narrative as a Social Symbolic Act*. London: Methuen, 1981.

Johnson, Pauline. *Marxist Aesthetics: The Foundations Within Everyday Life for an Emancipated Consciousness*. London: Routledge, 2011.

Kant, Immanuel. *Critique of Judgment*. Translated by James Creed Meredith. Oxford: Oxford University Press, 2008.

Lehman, Kim. "The Tricky Notion of 'Value' in the Arts." *The Conversation*, 24 November 2013. Accessed 21 July 2017. http://theconversation.com/the-tricky-notion-of-value-in-the-arts-20408.

Lifshitz, Mikhail. *The Philosophy of Art of Karl Marx*. Translated by Ralph B. Winn. New York: Critics Group, 1938.

Lukács, Georg. 'Realism in the Balance'. In *Aesthetics and Politics*, edited by Theodor Adorno et al. London: Verso, 2006.

Macherey, Pierre. *A Theory of Literary Production*. Translated by Geoffrey Wall. London: Routledge, 2006.

Marcuse, Hebert. *The Aesthetic Dimension*. Translated by Herbert Marcuse and Erica Sherover. London: Macmillan, 1979.

Marx, Karl. *Capital*. Edited by David McLellan. Oxford: Oxford University Press, 2008.

———. *The Civil War in France*. New York: International Publishers, 1940.

———. *The Class Struggle in France*. New York: International Publishers, 1964.

———. *Dispatches for the New York Tribune: Selected Journalism of Karl Marx*. Edited by James Ledbetter. London: Penguin Books, 2007.

———. *Early Writings*. Translated by Rodney Livingstone and Gregor Benton. London: Penguin, 1992.

———. *Economic and Philosophic Manuscripts of 1844*. Translated by Martin Milligan. Moscow: Progress Publishers, 1967.

———. *The Eighteenth Brumaire of Louis Napoleon*. Translated by D. D. L. New York: Mondial, 2005.

———. *Grundrisse: Foundations of the Critique of Political Economy*. Translated by Martin Nicolaus. London: Penguin Books, 1993.

———. 'Letter from Marx to Engels in Manchester'. *Marxist Internet Archive*. Accessed 21 January 2018. https://www.marxists.org/archive/marx/works/1869/letters/69_04_15-abs.htm.

———. 'On Freedom of the Press'. *Marxist Internet Archive*. Accessed 27 July 2017. https://www.marxists.org/archive/marx/works/1842/free-press/index.htm.

———. *The Poverty of Philosophy: Answer to the 'Philosophy of Poverty' by M. Proudhon*. Peking: Foreign Languages Press, 1978.

———. *Theories of Surplus Value*. Translated by G. A. Bonner and Emile Burns. London: Lawrence & Wishart, 1951.

———. *Theories of Surplus-Value*. *Marxist Internet Archive*. Accessed 14 January 2018. https://www.marxists.org/archive/marx/works/1863/theories-surplus-value.

Marx, Karl, and Friedrich Engels. *The Communist Manifesto*. Hammondsworth: Penguin Books, 1986.

———. *The German Ideology, including Theses on Feuerbach and Introduction to the Critique of Political Economy*. New York: Prometheus Books, 1998.

———. *The Holy Family: Critique of Critical Critique*. Honolulu: University Press of the Pacific, 2002.

———. *Marx & Engels on Literature and Art*. Edited by Lee Baxandall and Stefan Morawski. St Louis; Milwaukee: Telos Press, 1973.

Plato. *The Republic*. Translated by H. D. P. Lee. Harmondsworth: Penguin, 1960.

Prawer, S. S. *Karl Marx and World Literature*. Oxford: Oxford University Press, 1978.

Rancière, Jacques. *The Politics of Aesthetics*. Translated by Gabriel Rockhill. London: Bloomsbury, 2011.

Rose, Margaret A. *Marx's Lost Aesthetic: Karl Marx and the Visual Arts*. Cambridge: Cambridge University Press, 1984.

Ross, Kristin. *The Emergence of Social Space: Rimbaud and the Paris Commune*. London: Verso, 2007.

Rousseau, Jean-Jacques. *The Essential Rousseau*. Translated by Lowell Bair. New York: Mentor, 1974.

Trotsky, Leon. *Literature and Revolution*. Edited by William Keach. Chicago: Haymarket Books, 2005.

Williams, Raymond. *Marxism and Literature*. Toronto: Oxford University Press. 1977.

Wilson, Sarah. *Picasso/Marx and Socialist Realism in France*. Liverpool: Liverpool University Press, 2013.

Žižek, Slavoj. *The Sublime Object of Ideology*. London: Verso, 1995.

INDEX

abstract labour, 97
Adorno, Theodor, 119–120
advertisement, journalism as, 75–76
The Aesthetic Dimension (Marcuse),
    119
aesthetic regime of the arts, 10–11
aesthetics: beauty and, 68; Hegel on,
    32–34; Kant and, 32; Marx, K.,
    on, 68–69; Rousseau on, 29–30;
    surplus-value and, 82
Agamben, Giorgio, 4, 6–9, 10, 117
alienation: Agamben and, 127;
    Aristotle on, 25; Badiou and,
    126–127; in capitalism, 94, 97;
    Fischer and, 120–121; German
    Idealism on, 94; Marcuse and, 119;
    Marx, K., on, 92–103; religion and,
    97; spirituality and, 95–99
Althusser, Louis, 69n18, 122–123, 124
ancien régime, 58
anonymous journalism, 75
Aristotle, 16, 21, 86, 107; on catharsis,
    25–26, 86; Hegel and, 32, 33; Kant
    and, 30
Art and Value (Beech), 12
artistic configuration: Badiou and, 126;
    Kant and, 31
Arts21Magazine, 2

Arts Council England, 1–2
atheism, 28, 33
Athena, 100–109
Augustine of Hippo, 26–27; Hegel
    and, 33; Kant and, 30
"The Author as Producer" (Benjamin),
    119
authorized and unauthorized writers,
    45–47

Bacon, Francis, 68
Badiou, Alain, 10, 117, 134n50;
    inaesthetics of, 4–6, 126; Kant and,
    31; truth and, 6, 98, 126–127
Bakunin, Mikhail, 115
bankable artists, 13
Bauer, Bruno, 49, 50, 53
beauty: aesthetics and, 68; eternal law
    of, 49
Beech, Dave, 12
Benjamin, Walter, 119
Bennett, Tony, 15–16
Bonaparte, Louis-Napoléon, 76
bourgeois (ruling class), 53–69; capital
    of, 71–87; *The Civil War in France*
    and, 60–61; commodification by,
    93; *The Eighteenth Brumaire of
    Louis-Napoléon* and, 62;

ABOUT THE AUTHOR

Ali Alizadeh is a senior lecturer in literary studies and creative writing at Monash University's School of Languages, Literatures, Cultures and Linguistics. His books include collections of poems, *Towards the End, Ashes in the Air* and *Eyes in Times of War*; novels, *The Last Days of Jeanne d'Arc, Transactions* and *The New Angel*; and a work of literary nonfiction, *Iran, My Grandfather*. This is his first philosophical monograph.